50
SUCCESSFUL
HARVARD
BUSINESS
SCHOOL
APPLICATION
ESSAYS

Also by the Staff of The Harvard Crimson

50 SUCCESSFUL HARVARD BUSINESS SCHOOL APPLICATION ESSAYS

With Analysis by the Staff of *The Harvard Crimson*

ST. MARTIN'S GRIFFIN
NEW YORK

First published in the United States by St. Martin's Griffin, an imprint of St. Martin's Publishing Group

www.stmartins.com

Library of Congress Cataloging-in-Publication Data

Title: 50 successful Harvard Business School application essays : with analysis by the staff of the Harvard Crimson / The Staff of the Harvard Crimson.
Other titles: Fifty successful Harvard Business School application essays
Description: First edition. | New York : St. Martin's Griffin, 2022.
Identifiers: LCCN 2022026552 | ISBN 9781250845993 (trade paperback) | ISBN 9781250845986 (ebook)
Subjects: LCSH: Harvard Business School—Admission. | Business schools—Massachusetts—Admission. | College applications—Massachusetts. | Essay—Authorship. | Academic writing.
Classification: LCC HF1134.H4 A15 2022 | DDC 650.071/1744—dc23/eng/20220624
LC record available at https://lccn.loc.gov/2022026552

Our books may be purchased in bulk for promotional, educational, or business use. Please contact your local bookseller or the Macmillan Corporate and Premium Sales Department at 1-800-221-7945, extension 5442, or by email at MacmillanSpecialMarkets@macmillan.com.

First Edition: 2022

0 9 8 7 6 5 4 3 2 1

CONTENTS

I. Self-Reflection

II. Turning Adversity into Opportunity

Contents

Contents

ACKNOWLEDGMENTS

We would first like to thank our incredible team at *The Harvard Crimson* for their hard work: Sofia Diaz-Rodriguez, Amy Zhou, Cynthia Lu, Eric Elliott, Yab Demisie, Taia Cheng, Rhocar Constant, Maria De Los Santos, Westby Caspersen, Micheal Zhang, and Nathan Sun. We are also grateful to our business manager, Melissa Du, and our incredible editor at St. Martin's Press, Sallie Lotz, for her support. Lastly, we are so thankful for our fifty HBS contributors. Thank you for sharing your stories. We could not have done it without you.

—Isabelle Guillaume, Jenny Li, Shiyun Tang
Publishing Managers,
149th Guard of *The Harvard Crimson*

INTRODUCTION

The Admissions Essay

"As we review your application, what more would you like us to know as we consider your candidacy for the Harvard Business School MBA program?"

It's a daunting question. Open-ended and with no word limit, this prompt can seem impossible to answer.

Frankly, this book won't give you the answer. After reading these essays, you will see that there is no template for the perfect response. Each of the selected essays is completely different and personal to the writer—the essays themselves range from eight hundred to more than fourteen hundred words. Our selection by no means covers the extent of successful applicant essays, but they are united in their ability to showcase the writer's character.

In this book, we feature fifty successful applicants to the HBS MBA program. Each profile also includes analysis written by members of *The Harvard Crimson*, who highlight why each essay stands out and distill takeaways that can be used in your own essays.

This book won't tell you what to write, but we hope it will inspire you in your own process of self-reflection to take advantage of the prompt's open-endedness and make your essay your own. What more do you want the admissions team to know about yourself? Best of luck in finding out.

AUTHORS' NOTE

When writing the essay, the applicant may choose to disclose private parts of their life to the Admissions Committee. To respect all persons' and companies' privacy while maintaining the integrity of each essay, applicants had the option to choose aliases, disclose varying levels of background information, and redact identifying information with brackets ("[" and "]"). Edits have also been made to improve clarity or maintain anonymity. Thank you for your understanding.

I
SELF-REFLECTION

GRACE M.

Home State/Country: Tennessee, USA
Undergraduate School: University of Notre Dame
GPA Range: 3.3–3.7
GMAT: 750 T (45V; 48Q)
Work Experience: Private Equity
Word Count: 1,052

ESSAY

Since I was six, my family has volunteered to help the desperately poor and medically underserved in the remote village Boucan Carre, Haiti. Until my sisters and I were old enough to volunteer in Haiti ourselves, we would help from home, picking up donations, organizing annual benefits, and leading fundraisers. When I was fourteen, my parents fostered a Haitian boy, who was seeking medical treatment for growth hormone deficiency and malnutrition. Due to his condition, at the age of twelve, [he] stood three feet tall, weighed 45 pounds, and wore a 5T size in clothing. He was sweet and playful, but at times struggled to overcome anger, sorrow, and self-harm, resulting in violent and often public outbursts. We loved [him] despite the challenges, and our family adapted. My parents were, rightly, consumed with [him] and his well-being, so I embraced the role of mediator within our large family. I took on a parent role to my younger sister, who felt neglected, and I supported my parents to ease their burden. Though fostering [him] was difficult, we grew stronger as a family and in our relationships to both [him] and each other. I had expected to take on the role of older sister to [him], but I never anticipated that my role with my younger sister, or my parents, would change as well. Interpersonal relationships are complex and dynamic, and through the experience, I learned that a significant change to an established system, like my family, can create a ripple effect that can be difficult to predict.

In my professional experience, I have seen how targeted investments can have a similar unforeseen ripple effect on communities, positive or negative. For example, recent infrastructure investments by telecommunications companies have improved access to the internet in Africa, which has earned these companies higher subscriber growth, their intended outcome. The unintentional, although positive, ripple effect was that it paved the way for growth in digital finance in the region, giving millions of people access to credit and financial accounts who would not otherwise have them. Similarly, private equity has a place in the global economy as a stimulus for growth, innovation, and productivity, and also as a means to connect excess capital to companies seeking it. In my time at [Private Equity Firm], my team has invested in large companies based in South Korea, Germany, and the Netherlands. The investments have resulted in net job growth and productivity gains in their respective locations. However, the economic value of global investment activity and its ripple effect is not going far enough to affect villages like Boucan Carre or people like [my brother]. My hope is that with a deeper understanding of local cultural dynamics, international private equity investment can improve its impact and reach.

As a Lebanese-American growing up in a small Tennessee town, I learned to navigate the juxtaposed perspectives of my family in Lebanon and my environment in Knoxville and bridged the gap between the two cultures. Professionally, I have found that connecting across cultural divides is important for effective communication.

For example, I work closely with a company based in Seoul, and through interacting with colleagues there, I observed that professional culture in Korea is far more formal than in America. Drawing on my experience connecting my Lebanese and southern cultures, I trained my own mannerisms to improve our communication, even in minor ways such as referring to familiar colleagues as "Mr." or "Ms." By improving my awareness of cultural nuances and adapting my communication habits, our interactions became more effective and, eventually, more frequent, which helped information flow across the two groups.

I want to invest in international markets, where I can apply my skills in finance and my perspectives on relationships and working across cultures to make an impact on the poorest communities. Upon graduation, I want to join an operations-focused private equity firm with international reach, because investing in developing markets will be at a smaller scale than my work thus far at [Private Equity Firm] and will require more operations improvements to create value for individual communities.

To be successful in my goal, I need a broader business base. My education and career have been narrowly focused in finance and at arm's length. At my firm, we talk about the complexities of integrating acquisitions, but I have never integrated disparate IT systems myself or seen the work that goes into it. We tell our investors about operational improvements we can make, but I have never run manufacturing equipment or improved output. The next step to fill these gaps is to gain greater understanding in new areas of business. Based on my discussions with current students (e.g., [HBS Student] '19) and alumni (e.g., [HBS Alum] '16) who are colleagues, I know that HBS is the best program to attain this broader business base and to engage myself in a campus community. I will take advantage of courses such as Managing International Trade and

Investment to understand the landscape of foreign investment, and TOM to deepen my understanding of operations, an area in which I am weak today. I will learn from section mates from diverse backgrounds who view problems and approach solutions differently. I can apply my experiences to real-life scenarios in cases and group assignments. I hope to pursue a FIELD immersion program where, for example, my group could implement a new product in a developing community, execute a marketing strategy at a small scale in a foreign country, and confront real, localized problems in the process. I plan to join the Investment Club to learn from peers from other asset class backgrounds, like start-ups or international growth equity. There, I can leverage my experience leading Notre Dame's Wall Street Club by organizing speaker series around broader investment strategies, including social impact and emerging markets, which will develop my understanding of localized investing in international markets.

Private equity investment has the potential to positively impact communities like [my brother's]. By transcending cultural divides, investments can create opportunities that are mutually beneficial to local populations and businesses, creating jobs and new industries that improve quality of life for low-income communities, while being economically attractive for companies. I know HBS can deliver an MBA experience that provides me with the broad business foundation I need to be effective in targeted investing in developing markets.

ANALYSIS

Throughout her essay, Grace draws an interesting parallel between her personal and professional lives. She describes the profound impact of her family's fostering when she was fourteen, which fundamentally reshaped her relationship with and role among her family members. She learns here that "a significant change to an established system . . . can create a ripple effect."

The theme of a "ripple effect" reappears in her professional life. Grace outlines what her work entails: investing in various industries throughout developing countries, seeking to create employment opportunities, and elevating economic welfare. Grace talks about how such investments, even unintentionally, lead to various benefits in regional enterprises and promote overall well-being. Grace demonstrates her global character by highlighting various professional experiences around the world and ties this narrative back to Harvard Business School in relation to the professional skills she hopes to develop through the MBA program.

—Felipe Tancredo

Sidd B.

Home State/Country: United Arab Emirates
Undergraduate School: Columbia University
GPA Range: Undisclosed
GMAT: Undisclosed
Work Experience: Private Equity
Word Count: 1,097

ESSAY

The conspicuously large red glasses that have adorned my face for the past decade are integral to who I am. These 2″ x 2″ square-faced rims have proven to be an instant conversation starter and a means by which I am often remembered. They are even featured on a crowd-sourced page on WikiCU—Columbia's version of Wikipedia—meant to chronicle my work as Student Body President. In fact, my glasses have their own page too. All this attention, now endearing, to a pair of glasses was certainly never my intention. The red glasses resemble merely a fashionable accessory to most, but have a far deeper significance to me: they embody a past insecurity that I have now overcome.

Growing up in the desert city of Dubai, I have ironically always been attracted to water activities, and was a competitive swimmer during middle school. I loved the sport and used it as a channel to navigate what was a tough period of social identity. While I made many new friends at swim meets, I also truly valued the reflective time I had to myself in the pool. However, my vision started to deteriorate at the age of thirteen, and my parents introduced me to my first pair of remarkably average spectacles. Over the following eighteen months, my vision became blurrier and I would get throbbing headaches if I did not wear my glasses. Although significant astigmatism is not an uncommon condition, it was a weakness that constantly stared me in the face and seriously impacted my daily life. I questioned what I had done wrong and how I could counter what I viewed as a handicap—should I watch less TV? Should I change my vegetarian diet? Should I pray more frequently at the temple?

My vision disadvantaged me in the pool, and I slowly lost interest in swimming. It was agonizing to find myself distant from such an important part of my childhood. I acknowledged that the plastic frame with thick lenses was here to stay. To a younger version of myself, it seemed like I was destined to parade my weakness perched on my nose with no place to hide.

After a year of resentment, I was poised to shake things up. I was determined to tackle this demon and reimagine the implications. On a summer trip to Mumbai, I purchased my first pair of jumbo unbranded red glasses. The large size and loud color were a deliberate choice. This was my internal battle cry as I was tired of hiding—no more drab glasses; no more shunning my handicap.

The principal back at my conservative high school disliked the bright red color that starkly contrasted with the somber school uniform, and was vocal about his distaste for the glasses. He attempted to bully me into not wearing them, but I was not willing to turn back now. My creative compromise was to resort to dual identities; I brought two pairs of glasses to school daily—the lively red pair for the classroom and a rimless sober pair for the common areas that the principal roamed.

Fortunately, college was more welcoming; "are they real?" was the third most frequent question during orientation after "how do you speak such fluent English?" and "did you ride camels back home?" My red glasses were an easy icebreaker and the unconventional fashion appeal helped debunk stereotypes of an engineer's appearance. The warm response towards my red glasses gave me newfound confidence in my new home many seas away from family. This self-belief helped me successfully run for freshman Class Representative, which subsequently led to three reelections in different capacities on student council. My team and our agenda evolved each year but the constant red glasses portrayed a sense of familiarity and trustworthiness. The red glasses accompanied my team on our posters around campus, on our social media outreach, and as we went door to door speaking with the constituents we strived to serve. Even those that were unaware of the student council's initiatives knew they could always reach out to "the guy with red glasses." Inadvertently, the red glasses had become my personal brand.

As I embarked into the business world, I gave considerable thought to how I would present myself. Post college, pressed suits and ties replaced t-shirts and sweatpants, and I questioned if I was supposed to retire the red glasses for a more professional alternative. Recalling my high school experience, I settled on a dual appearance, wearing different sets of glasses depending on my target audience and desired message. While this helped me control my persona, the glasses were still more of a trusted friend than simply a showpiece; they continued to give me courage and reminded me not to back down in challenging times. In my first year at [the investment firm], I spent a couple months at my portfolio company and the experience was initially as uncomfortable as it was exciting. I had to often provide guidance to senior executives who were far more tenured than I was, and I questioned how I, three years into my career, was to convince industry experts of my views. Through my internal conflict, the red glasses I wore served as a constant reminder that I could push through my reservations, and I did.

My red glasses have become endearing to friends and family because they are truly an extension of myself. Friendly, colorful, and bold, they encapsulate my personality well. Friends (and occasionally strangers) often grabbed my glasses to take a photograph wearing them, leading to a photography blog through senior year of college titled "Sidd B. Imposters" that captured over a hundred such moments. After years of practice, I even have a jovial response to compliments now: "Thanks—they're the only reason I have friends!"

As an investment professional today, I look back and realize that the red glasses have yielded an unexpectedly high return on investment; they seem to have an intangible draw that enhances what I bring to the table. Accompanying me on my journey thus far, the red glasses are essential to my individuality. They have become what my family and friends expect to be greeted with, give me a mode to connect with strangers, and reinforce the boldness I feel we should all have towards our work and dreams. Although I aspire to wear crimson red proudly, I have no intention of leaving behind my candy apple red glasses. I am confident that they will help me embrace the dreaded cold call and will partake in the many adventures I hope to have with my section mates.

ANALYSIS

This essay exemplifies how seemingly small moments can be told in big ways. Sidd begins the essay by introducing his red glasses as a symbol of personal growth and uniqueness. Instead of viewing his vision as a handicap, Sidd accepts it and his glasses as part of his identity. This association between Sidd and the glasses establishes a strong hook and provides a symbol that he is able to refer back to throughout the essay.

Sidd parallels the red glasses with his evolution towards self-acceptance and openness to new experiences. Sidd uses the glasses as a token to remind himself of his ability to overcome limitations and become a better student and professional. Through these stories, Sidd is also able to present his professional accomplishments and strong work experience. By presenting his experiences and accomplishments through the theme of the red glasses, Sidd was able to craft a compelling narrative essay.

—Felipe Tancredo

Alexis R.

Home State/Country: USA
Undergraduate School: University of Wisconsin-Madison
GPA Range: 3.3–3.7
GMAT: 700 T (40V; 45Q)
Work Experience: Corporate Finance
Word Count: 1,305

ESSAY

The past year has been one of much introspection for me. I've looked internally to understand my motivations, what's important to me, and how my past experiences have shaped me for future success. Through this time of reflection, I've concluded that going back to school to pursue my MBA at HBS is the ultimate next step, not only to build upon the professional I am today, but more broadly, to collectively better myself as a person.

As grounding, I'll start with where I've been.

My name is Alexis R. I was born in North Dakota and moved to Wisconsin when I was ten years old. I grew up in Appleton, Wisconsin, as an only child of two parents that taught me the importance of hard work, persistence, and staying true to your Vikings roots in the heart of Green Bay Packer country. My parents instilled in me the power of determination and commitment, and I modeled myself after them in my definition of success.

After graduating from college, I began work full-time at a large CPG company, and the experience thus far has challenged and grown me more than I would have ever expected. Finance is at the epicenter of all business; a reputable colleague that other functions lean on for advice and counsel. Two years out of school, I sat on the leadership team of one of our Customer Sales Regions, the sole Finance support for the Sales team. I played an exciting role above my experience as the trusted adviser to my Senior Sales Director. We worked together to make things happen quickly, and I was able to influence decisions due to her trust in my abilities. I admired the action-oriented, motivating style with which this woman led, and it was something I focused on building within myself.

My next rotation brought me to the Cereal Operating Unit, where I was the Finance point for Cereal Innovation. I led the financial modeling and analytics for numerous successful new product launches, all of which taught me the strength in operating through ambiguity and working quickly to resolution rather than dwelling on a problem. This role was also my first glance into the power of true business partnership—I learned the underlying motivations that guided the decisions my business partners were making, and I was able to use this as a solid foundation to influence the team and provide direction. Chocolate Peanut Butter Oats was a project that portrayed these underlying motivations very clearly. Product engineers wanted to use tasty, high-cost ingredients, while Consumer Insights wanted a healthier nutrition label. Supply Chain wanted one singular carton size to reduce complexity, while Sales wanted three to ensure strong distribution. This was my opportunity to truly make an impact—I was able to contextualize the trade-offs for the team and educate them on the important role that Innovation played in the Operating Unit's long-range plan. It was through my high degree of business partnership that I was able to bring Finance to the forefront and ensure that we had all the context necessary to make the right decisions.

I then moved into my current role in North America Planning

and Analysis. This has given me a completely different set of skills as I build capabilities to analyze results and understand drivers of change. In this role, I provide direction and insights to the President and VP of Finance for our North America business. I get the opportunity to sit with these senior leaders and hear the questions they're asking, the trade-offs they're making, and the recommendations and decisions they own. It is through this experience that I've learned the significance of simplicity. Complexity leads to confusion, and the leaders I look up to are able to see the complexity, understand it, and then relay it in a concise, easy-to-interpret way. The power of leading with simplicity is often overlooked but is something I value considerably.

As I review the career moments that have developed who I want to be as a leader, it's important to note two other influential parts of my life outside of work: my time as a Big Sister as part of the Big Brothers Big Sisters program and my experience as a volunteer tax preparer with Prepare + Prosper, a nonprofit organization focused on increasing the community's financial wellness. I have been a Big for the past five years and came into the program hoping to make a lasting impact on a young girl's life. What I have found instead is that while my impact on my Little's life is valuable, the pieces that she has taught me have already had a lasting effect on my own life. She has taught me the importance of staying curious, how to be more patient, and how different values drive different behaviors. I have also been a volunteer tax preparer for the past five years for low-income local residents. I can't count the number of tax returns I've filed that have had donations to charity in an income bracket lower than the poverty line or the number of clients who have thanked me incessantly for my services even after a multi-hour wait. I see the selflessness and gratitude of these people, with backgrounds different than my own, and have learned to truly appreciate what I can gain from others. It is through these relationships that I've discovered that to be a respected leader, empathy and an understanding of how others operate is as important as, if not more than, the analytical skills I've naturally developed.

Through my roles at my previous employer as well as the activities that occupy my time outside of the office, it is clear that my past has formulated the way I think about my future. With that in mind, I am at a point in my career where I am shifting from grounding myself in detailed financial analysis to more forward-thinking, strategic recommendations and decisions. To aid in this shift, I need to fully envelop myself in the focus on that goal. As I've progressed through my career, I've always received high praise for my analytical capabilities and my ability to partner with the team to create actionable next steps. Although, I have admittedly not been the loudest at the table. Colleagues respect and trust my abilities and have mentioned that they'd like to hear even more from me. I take time to gather my thoughts and formulate my opinion with 100% certainty before voicing it outwardly. Through my own internalization of this feedback, I am now more focused than ever to make the change; to move from analytical horsepower to leading the discussion and influencing the outcome. This determination has bolstered my decision to make a solid commitment to self-improvement, lively debate and discussion, and ensuring that my voice is heard. It is through HBS's program that I can accelerate my leadership goals. It is the case method that provides the perfect backdrop for taking often ambiguous, complex data and boiling it down into succinct direction. It is the highly verbal environment that provides a learning ground for my desire to speak my mind more quickly and partner with others of unique and diverse backgrounds. It is the talented classmates around me that provide insights into what it takes to motivate and lead to action. All of this culminates into my notion of the impact I'll make on the world. On my path to becoming a leader in the CPG industry, I desire to bring tangible happiness to consumers through the products I trust and believe in, all while being a highly motivating leader deeply grounded in the values I was raised upon. HBS is the next step in that path forward for me; a mutually beneficial relationship that will foster both personal development and professional success.

ANALYSIS

Alexis paints a vivid picture of life experiences that have brought her to apply to Harvard Business School. Alexis opens with how she was raised on hard work and persistence, and she carries these values throughout her life and this essay.

By contextualizing various parts of her experience in the CPG industry, the reader has a better grasp of the importance of each activity and the lessons that she has learned. Alexis also highlights her volunteer experiences in the Big Brothers Big Sisters program and Prepare + Prosper, which sets her apart from other candidates who might focus solely on work experience. By showing that her values align with future aspirations, Alexis clearly expresses why she would be a good fit for Harvard Business School.

—Yab Demisie

SUHAYL C.

Home State/Country: New York, USA
Undergraduate School: Georgetown University
GPA Range: 3.3–3.7
GMAT: 760 T (46V; 49Q)
Work Experience: Consulting
Word Count: 1,027

ESSAY

"I've been thinking of making the journey to Europe, you know, as a refugee." My friend dropped the sentence on our dinner like a lead paperweight, and the guilt started to settle in: I would never have to make such a terrible choice in my entire life. Having also lived as a gay man in the Middle East for several years, I was intimately familiar with many of the challenges: the public restrictions on affection, the lack of legal rights, the familial pressures. But I could move freely; the luxury of being born with an American passport meant I could live and find opportunity wherever I wanted—a luxury I had taken for granted.

[My friend], born and raised in Baghdad, had been living for years in Dubai (UAE) working for an international company, so he had a comfortable life and financial independence. However, it was always on his mind how quickly his situation could change: UAE visas are linked to work, so if he lost his job, got sick or injured, his only option would be to return to the violence and stagnation of Iraq—and back to being dependent on a traditional (homophobic) family. However, applying for asylum was equally fraught: it meant forfeiting his money and savings, living in camps, separated from his family and friends, potentially years until he would be able to work and travel again. No matter what path he chose, he would have to sacrifice something critical. A tough choice for anyone, but especially for a young gay Arab; he told me he couldn't forfeit the prospect of a future where he could live openly as an equal in society, so he gave up everything and put behind his past life, fleeing to Finland.

I had been aware of my privilege—education, passport, etc.—but it wasn't until that day that I really internalized how much that determined what choices and opportunities I would have in life. I had doors open to me that [my friend] would never be able to walk through. I was struck not just by the magnitude of the differences in opportunity between us, but by how arbitrary it was, how much it was created by historical trends and decisions made by people years before we were born rather than through the decisions we'd made in life, how with just a few different choices in our family histories our positions could easily be reversed.

It had a profound effect on how I see the world and what drives me towards leadership; it is the reason I am applying to get my MBA from HBS. It taught me that I have the responsibility to seize the opportunities available to me and use them to challenge structures that perpetuate inequalities and create opportunities for others. So much of what determines what paths are available to whom is beyond our individual capacity; having the privilege to develop the knowledge and capabilities needed to become a global leader is a gift that is not to be wasted.

At the same time, there has never been a greater need for visionary leadership to guide us through major societal issues: the excesses of capitalism, income inequality, environmental destruction, and so on. Major change will not come from outside the core system of business and profit; business must be part of any sustainable solution to the problems facing humanity. And so, as business leaders we must take it upon ourselves to think beyond the quarterly profits and find solutions for how to make profits align with a sustainable human future. This is what matters most to me: finding profitable ways to make capitalism less exploitative and improving the structures of society to be more just and equitable.

In my career, this has so far meant creating opportunities for people who are structurally disadvantaged. I spent the past two years using my drive towards meaningful impact to build SINGA Business Lab, an inclusive incubator encouraging innovation and entrepreneurship among refugees and new arrivals to Europe. The experience truly opened my mind beyond the intellectual bubble of management consulting and taught me several valuable lessons beyond the entrepreneurial journey of building something new from the ground up. I saw directly the impact of being given an opportunity and how much this can change a life. I learned the difficulty of effecting wide scale structural change from the non-profit world and this convinced me of the need to lead change from within our existing economic structures. And finally, I came to deeply understand the truly transformative power of technology today, how rapid innovation enables us to create change more rapidly and at a larger scale than ever before.

This drive and these experiences have helped me define the leader I want to be: values driven, identifying the links between better business and a better society to lead my organization to where we can push beyond our limits. In this world, there are many [Friend Name]s whose lives have placed them in lose-lose situations, while only a few get the opportunity to lead. So those of us that do get this opportunity have a responsibility to make things better for those that do not. Driven by the knowledge not just of my own friend, but by how many millions there are like him, I want to lead businesses that harness the power of new technology to create opportunities for others and build a society better for all.

To become this kind of leader, an HBS MBA is the clear next step for me. HBS is the apex of business education, and would put me much closer to achieving these goals. Beyond the world-class curriculum, I would be immersed in a student body of some of the most intelligent people on earth—people I can learn from, and a global network that will also enable more impact in the future—and in an unmatched intellectual atmosphere. I am confident that nowhere would be able to teach me to be the kind of leader that I would learn at HBS, and it is these kinds of leaders that make the change I want to make in the world.

ANALYSIS

In this essay, Suhayl drives home not only the reason why he chose Harvard Business School but also why he would be a good match for the school. At the beginning, Suhayl paints a vivid picture of his home situation and presents a problem that his friend and by extension Suhayl are facing. By doing this, he provides the reader with a glimpse of his background and obstacles this background creates.

This also helps create a sense of how Suhayl will use his HBS education. While he explicitly states at the end how he will use his degree, these points are already previewed and implied in the body of the essay when he describes how his experiences led him to create the business lab to address the many disparities and problems he saw in the world. This allows the reader to get the sense that this actionability will translate from this experience over to Harvard Business School and into the real world.

One of the most striking features of this essay is the author's acknowledgment of his privilege. Suhayl explains to the reader that while his experience is starkly different from his friend's because of his American citizenship, he still sees and understands the problems that others face. Suhayl also acknowledges that he could very easily have that same fate if a few things had been different in his past. This acknowledgment is emotionally impactful and allows the reader to see the author's humble but entrepreneurial personality through his work. When Suhayl later ties it into why he wants to be at Harvard Business School, the reader has the context to how his work has been impactful for himself and his community.

—Yab Demisie

NISHA D.

Home State/Country: Florida, USA
Undergraduate School: University of Pennsylvania
GPA Range: 3.3–3.7
GMAT: 760 T (44V; 49Q)
Work Experience: Private Equity
Word Count: 1,318

ESSAY

I was 4 years old when I stepped foot in my first Bharatnatyam dance class. Everything was foreign to me—I had just learned how to walk a couple years back, and now this? But the moment the girls' feet struck the floor, I was mesmerized by the way their movement captured a steady rhythm. I galloped over to the others in excitement and gave it a try. Right. Left. Jump. Right. In that simple moment, I was hooked. Bharatnatyam, though best known for its powerful footwork and elegant storytelling, is also described as a brutal test of stamina, commitment, and grit, not typically suited for someone who hasn't even hit puberty. My parents assumed I would eventually get fed up and quit like most others who caved under the pressure. However, the rush I felt as a toddler kept me hypermotivated for the next 7 years as I trained for my Arangetram, the coveted two-hour solo graduation performance.

The path to the finish line was not an easy one. I struggled in areas that required maturity, such as extension, emotion, and stage presence, and I often felt inadequate versus my older peers. I practiced twice as hard for months, going so far as to tell myself stories with just my eyes while brushing my teeth to improve my expressions. At age 11, I beat the odds and became the youngest dancer in Central Florida to receive her diploma. As I took my final bow that evening, I realized my first experience as a dancer not only tested my character—it defined it. The ruthless discipline I developed at an early age from dance naturally bled over into all areas of my life, which pushed me to achieve a unique well-roundedness. An example of a day in my high school shoes looked like this: 5 A.M. wake-up, debate team captains meeting during lunch, Latin ballroom competition run-through after school, pit stop at Taco Bell with friends, Spanish homework, evening tennis practice, Indian soap operas with grandma, sleep. My friends questioned whether I really did that last step, but my trick never involved skipping my beauty sleep. My secret sauce was the way I was hardwired as a dancer; I was laser focused on putting more than I thought I had into every new venture to leave a lasting impact rather than simply "learning the moves."

Over the years, I gained fluency in balancing several moving pieces at once and was thrilled to receive the "Best Dancer" senior superlative, to be appointed captain of my varsity tennis team, and even to strut down the football field as "Homecoming Princess." As I stood at the podium to give my graduation speech as valedictorian, I was proud, but I was even prouder to have become someone the athletes, student government leaders, artists, and other multi-faceted students sitting across from me could relate to and respect. I entered Penn feeling like a rock star, but I was quickly humbled when I noticed my individual efforts, no matter how disciplined, weren't getting me very far. I struggled in my first Economics class. I got rejected from several on-campus organizations I applied to. And when I finally landed my first leadership position with the South Asia Society (SAS), the group was dysfunctional and uninvolved.

As I examined what I could possibly do to turn SAS around, dance once again proved to be my fail-safe. My college dance team, Penn Masti, taught me the importance of collaboration and camaraderie for a group's success—after all, if one member was unprepared or disinterested, our practices lost productivity and our performances unraveled. Ergo, for the next three years on SAS Board, I poured my energy into building an analogously positive culture and sense of community. I launched several team-building initiatives, including an annual retreat, one-on-one coffee chats, monthly Board bonding events, and "Highs and Lows" exercises, and gradually the culture improved. For the first time ever, I saw bonds and passion form that sparked new ideas for programming and growth. Over time, we attracted a tight-knit network of 300+ students that became one of the most active and influential communities on campus.

Though this was my first real experience as a member of a high-functioning team, it transformed my toolkit for an approach to my career in finance. A few months into my job in healthcare investment banking, the most senior banker in our office quit, along with 5 others. The group left behind was severely under-resourced and overwhelmed. Right on cue, at the worst possible time, I got an offer to start early at my current job. The idea of leaving my group hanging during a time of extremely low team morale kept me up every night. If I left, I could burn bridges with the same people who developed me. But if I stayed, I could stall my career. I ultimately chose to stay with my team. My decision forced me to step up to positions above my level given our limited human capital. I put in several 4 A.M. nights digesting research on cell therapy, building meticulous market models, and practicing presentations to executives to close one of the most transformative biotech deals of 2017. My dance discipline kept me going despite the 100-hour workweeks. It also drove me to simultaneously help reinvigorate my team. I offered a listening ear to disgruntled analysts who wanted to see change. I organized weekly team lunches and a transparent staffing sheet to streamline workflow communication. I even recruited talented new analysts to solidify the sustainability of the group. Very slowly, but surely, the group emerged from the slump as a cohesive unit, and I moved on having gained valuable deal experience and knowing they were well-equipped to handle future obstacles together.

I, much to my chagrin, admit that since graduating I've been consumed on multiple occasions with the rigorous single focus of work. I find myself battling with time while trying to balance my professional ambitions in healthcare private equity with my personal goals—sometimes it feels as though there aren't enough hours in a day. Dance has thankfully been my avenue to escape and connect with my community. Upon moving to New York, I was eager to blend my passion for dance with my desire to build meaningful relationships outside of work. I began volunteering for Dance for PD, a nonprofit offering specialized dance classes for patients with Parkinson's Disease to enhance cognition, motor skills, and social interaction. Swing dancing with 65-year-olds may not be the ideal Saturday morning for all, but I feel a fulfilling connection with my partner each time a hand stops trembling, or a smile emerges when he or she finds the beat. For everything dance has given me, it's been a privilege to help improve the well-being of others through dance. Even still, I've gained so much from this experience, perhaps most importantly learning resilience from my new companions who show up to every class with tales of last week's adventures in hand, as if no neurological condition stands between them and a normal lifestyle.

My first foray into dance was the beginning of the rest of my life as I know it. Dance empowered me to have no resistance whatsoever to hard work and taught me countless lessons that have made me the woman I am today. Today, I am more balanced, open-minded, and patient. Today, I believe that collaboration, or lack thereof, can catalyze leaders to either change the world or take a backseat. Looking forward, I am hopeful to make an impact at HBS and at a high-growth healthcare start-up with the same creative mindset and commitment to action. And though I can't be completely sure of what the future holds, I know I will always have a part of that little girl of 4 years within me—my love for dancing and everything it inspires me to do.

ANALYSIS

Nisha intertwines the imagery of her passion for dance with her personal and professional experiences to create a compelling narrative on resilience. Her narration on how Bharatnatyam "bled" into the different facets of her life and defined her character sets the foundation for the thesis: how dance formed her experiences and character. This is not only a beautiful thesis but also a strong motif, which becomes woven throughout the entire essay.

Nisha begins with her accomplishments in Bharatnatyam dance and then transitions into her high school experiences. Using the anchor of dance, Nisha explains how she does not "simply" learn the moves but also gives her all into every opportunity. She contrasts her high school successes, such as valedictorian and Homecoming Princess, with the struggles she faced starting college at the University of Pennsylvania. She also demonstrates the resilience taught to her through dance. This is further exemplified by her beginning workforce experiences—despite being given the opportunity to leave, Nisha decides to stay to bring back the success of the team. She illustrates the long workweeks, talent recruitment, and workflow communication she innovated in order to foster success.

Near the end of the essay, Nisha brings the story full circle by describing her volunteer work, emphasizing how dance taught her not only resilience but also how to make meaningful relationships, demonstrating her ability to balance life and connect with others.

Throughout this essay, Nisha proves her resilience, dedication, and passion to connect and collaborate with others. This narrative demonstrates to the admissions officers how effectively Nisha will use her MBA and what type of mark she wants to leave in her future endeavors in the health care field.

—Daniel Kwon

SEAN H.

Home State/Country: Texas, USA
Undergraduate School: Stanford University
GPA Range: 3.3–3.7
GRE: 331 T (164V; 167Q)
Work Experience: Consulting
Word Count: 1,202

ESSAY

When some people hear the word "jazz," they visualize a sensual club scene, while others see their grandfather in his rocking chair. Some imagine a band marching through the French Quarter, and yet others an underground rebellion. When I hear it, I think of identity, belonging, and me. The word authentically defines who I am and what I strive to achieve.

Jazz is the epitome of harmonizing and improvising unlikely, diverse motifs to create something new. Born into the center of jazz in New Orleans, my family is a mixture of Black and French, doctors and hustlers, musicians and accountants. Regardless of experience, we all come together as a family. This notion of jazz helps me determine what matters most to me—to create a sense of community and belonging for all people, especially for those who feel marginalized. To me, jazz is inherently entrepreneurial, and I strive to use this mindset to create more inclusive organizations.

This act of creating belonging, however, remains constantly challenged. Growing up in a southern, mostly white community as a lighter-complexioned Black person, I was ashamed of who I was, feeling like I didn't belong. My best friend in kindergarten casually said to me one day, "You know, 100 years ago I would've owned you." While I'm certain he was oblivious to the significance of his bigoted remark, the idea of being property, being innately less valuable than him, caused me to erect a wall inside.

This sense of non-belonging extended through college and into the professional world. During my internship in tech, I was the only Black person in my building. At my consulting job, I overheard analysts and managers alike question the value of diversity and inclusion programs like the ones that helped me obtain my jobs. Examining why I sometimes feel I don't belong in my own country, countless stories of Black people being murdered and vilified as "thugs" perpetuate fear and signal our existence as second-class citizens.

With the nonstop bombardment of these negative narratives, I painfully understand why Black people like me enter professional spaces with chips on our shoulders, knowing our validity is constantly being challenged. Thus, the question that perpetually drives me is how can I feel like I belong? How can I create inclusive environments for others?

I had the opportunity to answer this question during an internship at a FinTech company in Ghana. Still grappling with my identity, I selected Sub-Saharan Africa for my internship hoping to foster pride in my Blackness and serve my ancestral community. I immediately found myself in a welcoming environment, but still felt "othered"—not because of my race, but because of my complexion. People were genuinely, albeit politely, confused by my appearance, curious how I could have kinky hair but light skin. I would often hear the word "oburoni," meaning "wicked one," a remnant phrase of the slave trade that now simply means "white person." There I was—in a Black country searching for my Black heritage, only to be labeled a wicked white person.

In jazz, when someone misses a note or falls off-key, rather than see it as a mistake, we appreciate the nuance as part of the creative genesis, expanding the notion of what we define as "off." In this spirit and refusing to accept this rejection, I persisted on my journey to find community. I noticed at Hubtel that many employees seemed to share my feeling of isolation, and the physical environment exacerbated the issue. The building walls were prison grey, the lights were never on, the desks were cramped; there was no life or common identity. In addition to my assigned projects, I took the initiative to interview over 100 of Hubtel's employees to understand their passions, their communities, and what they felt was missing. True inclusion is the expansion of one's empathetic horizon to find commonality in new ways. Through listening to my coworkers' stories, we each connected through shared experiences, passions, and ideas.

Concretely, I also responded to their concerns of isolation by knocking down walls, repainting rooms, and transforming the office into a more "jazzy" creative space conducive to community engagement and productivity. I established weekly chats with the CEO where people could speak candidly about their work and the direction of the firm. Most importantly, I set up an informal HR system that validated the employees' voices, where they now felt they had a say in the company's products and strategic vision.

In just a few days, the environment changed completely. We began enjoying company dinners at employees' homes, and by the end of the summer, employees were actually staying at the office significantly longer (16%). They felt like the company now served as a community space where they belonged—I felt like I belonged, too.

By having the humility and initiative to empathize with people and authentically listen to their ideas and stories, I discovered commonality that evolved into community.

People became more understanding of me as a friend who believes in them and values the company's mission, rather than as an "oburoni" trying to appropriate their culture. True to the idea of jazz, we all brought a part of our unique selves to create something new. Hubtel revealed to me the power of belonging and how I can apply this familial notion of jazz in small social circles and on a global scale. However, the experience also highlighted how I merely scratched the surface in the value and Insight I could have provided, and that I have much more to learn and explore.

I absolutely loved being at the forefront of strategic change for a firm that continues to positively empower its community, and I want to continue this intellectual exploration of organizational theory, strategy, and macroeconomic change through business. I aspire to join the HBS family to bridge this knowledge gap and to better prepare myself to design inclusive environments and serve the entrepreneurial and strategic needs of underprivileged and developing Black communities, both domestically and internationally.

As an SVMP alumnus, Harvard has demonstrated to me that it can provide the tools I need to make an impact in these communities while also following my intellectual curiosities in organizational behavior, technology, and entrepreneurship. HBS is actually a lot like jazz, an environment known for improvising and breaking molds. The case method's focus on experiential learning serves as a perfect springboard for inclusive group discussions to identify solutions. Through the global-oriented FIELD program, the elements of inclusion, strategic improvisation, and diverse culture—all integral parts of my identity—are celebrated by the Harvard community.

As America's community and values continue to be tested by sentiments of racism and systemic injustice, I continue to remind myself of my beautiful cultural heritage and how I learned to be proud of who I am. Jazz did not arise easily from stories of happiness and trivial amalgamation; it emerged from grit and the perseverance of marginalized people coming together no matter the obstacle. In my life, and in my aspiration to be a part of the Harvard community, I remain dedicated to live up to the model of my ancestors and to expand the boundaries of belonging—to compose jazz.

"Profiles of Promise," https://www.youtube.com/watch?v=xrz9egdeQVc

ANALYSIS

Sean hooks readers by contesting the standard definition of jazz with his own personal meaning. Sean establishes that while he strives to use an entrepreneurial, jazz-inspired mindset to create more inclusive organizations, his identity in their community created a sense of non-belonging.

In the body of his essay, Sean speaks about his experience working at an internship in Ghana, where he noticed many employees felt isolated. Relating back to his goal of creating inclusive environments, he describes an initiative he undertook to foster community in the workplace, highlighting both his commitment to his goals and his individual drive and leadership skills.

Similar to jazz, Sean brought together a group of unique individuals to create a new sense of community. Sean concedes the experience only scratched the surface of the amount of change he could have provided and resolves that attending business school will bridge the knowledge gap necessary to serve underprivileged and developing communities. Returning to his theme of jazz, Sean concludes with a vow to remain dedicated to his goals, just like the grit and perseverance required to create the first jazz music.

Sean does not seem defeated by his challenging circumstances but instead shares an experience that highlights his ability to identify problems and confront them head-on to develop a solution. His background explains to admissions officers why he is interested in business school and showcases his commitment to improve inclusivity and community.

—Eric Elliott

HAILEY S.

Home State/Country: Connecticut, USA
Undergraduate School: The University of North Carolina
at Chapel Hill
GPA Range: 3.7–4.0
GRE: 327 T (159V; 168Q)
Work Experience: Consulting
Word Count: 999

ESSAY

Growing up as a competitive dancer, I sought to deeply understand
my teammates' personalities in order to improve communication,
build comradery, and perform our best onstage. I enjoyed learning about the specific choreography pieces that spoke to them and
including those components in our routine, enabling each person
to find joy in their performance. Although I'm no longer choreo-
graphing, I've continued to emphasize the importance of strong
communication channels in my professional endeavors. Until
my grandfather's passing, I thought my professional passions were
rooted in retail's digital disruption. I was fascinated with how technology improved the holistic retail experience. However, as my
grandfather battled dementia, I witnessed the information asymmetries that plague the U.S. healthcare system. Due to a data miscommunication amongst his physicians, he endured an erroneous
resuscitation, which resulted in a great deal of preventable pain and
his subsequent passing.

The jarring realization that an industry worth 18% of our GDP was so technologically behind shifted my professional focus towards addressing the communication inadequacies besieging health- care. Many doctors aren't given the data they need and are often rushed to the next patient, fostering an error-prone environment that pushes for the quickest, rather than the best, care. After observing my grandfather's complications, it became my mission to challenge the information and communication inaccuracies of the U.S. healthcare system, refusing to believe that an industry worth so much could let patients down so frequently. Thousands of patients die annually from preventable errors and nearly 5% of diagnoses are incorrect altogether. As hospitals purchase independent medical practices and leverage more at-home services, the need for streamlined communication will only increase.

In order to help tackle the communications issues that providers face, I aim to work as a VP of Product at a leading hospital system. I will focus on making information more actionable by developing products that better integrate data from patient health records. Leading my consulting team through the launch of a Medicare business, I discovered a niche curiosity for the challenges providers face when communicating internally; unfortunately, the status quo is adversely affecting patients. As our team designed a hospital discharge workflow, we observed doctors transitioning responsibilities to the discharge team, who sometimes didn't have the right information to discharge patients. Concerningly, patients often left the hospital without the best care plan or equipment to promote a healthy recovery. We saw how providers are stretched thin, burned out, and left without the right tools and data to provide high-quality care.

Additionally, hospitals' antiquated processes, such as lack of technology adoption and excessive regulatory restrictions, hinder rapid transfer of information, often impeding the smaller, innovative companies who want to not only send information quickly, but make it more actionable. Recalling my grandfather's experience, I knew this issue wasn't restricted to just insurance. The internal communication problems affected doctors' offices, hospitals, and other facets of the industry. An opportunity remains to disrupt the provider's experience by bridging this communication gap. I want to streamline provider workflows by developing better internal communication products that leverage patient health records. I will draw upon my experience in healthcare technology roles to enable more efficient product implementation, especially as it pertains to increasing the speed and accuracy of effective information transfer. My time at this company has allowed me to grasp a deeper understanding of the industry, enabling me to see that this communication problem is systemic and affects other stakeholders in the U.S. healthcare ecosystem.

Furthermore, I continue to witness the issues that start-ups endure given the slow implementation rate that legacy organizations face, specifically hospitals. Confronted with this issue early on, I led the team through a strategic pivot of our business model. I executed the cost-benefit analysis that moved our focus away from hospitals and towards independent medical practices, which also experience various information asymmetries due to their smaller size and budgets. While this has proven beneficial for our growth, I question how often this happens with smaller players in the industry and what hospitals, providers, and, most importantly, patients are missing out on as a result. My experience has shown me that I want to bridge this information and communication gap at a broader scale by working with a hospital system that has bought independent medical practices and has started to enhance their at-home services. I seek to prepare myself to be an executive in the space, one that leads with passion and fortitude to tackle the industry's greatest communication challenges in a way that appeals to business, provider, and consumer stakeholders. In transitioning to a product management role at a hospital, I will use the skills learned in my consulting and operational roles to drive change in an environment that hasn't, until fairly recently, been on the cutting edge of technology.

However, I understand that developing certain technical skill sets will be imperative in order to deeply understand the intricacies of the healthcare system and drive decisions alongside minds from business, clinical, technological, and political backgrounds. I will immerse myself in areas that challenge my perspectives with regard to formulating strategy, analyzing unstructured data, and managing technological and operational change in order to best position myself to lead within my organization and further my healthcare career. An HBS MBA will give me the technical skills required to analyze prior market decisions to inform future strategies and challenge this convoluted healthcare system alongside innovative thinkers. While my grandfather's experience is in the past, I'm committed to reducing miscommunication errors within hospitals and increasing information sharing amongst providers to alleviate these issues for other patients. Drawing upon my learnings as a young dancer, I'll enable my teams to develop products that bridge the communication gap and put joy back into care delivery for the provider. I will continuously seek to be at the forefront of healthcare innovation where I can launch products that invert the communication status quo of an archaic model—one that no longer meets the needs of the 21st century provider or patient.

ANALYSIS

Hailey begins the essay with a hook about how past work as a choreographer and dancer has taught her the value of teamwork and communication—values that she incorporates into her professional life. Aside from drawing the reader in, this anecdote establishes the eloquence of her clear communication style from the very beginning of the essay.

In the body of the essay, Hailey goes on to share memories of her grandfather's struggle with dementia and how miscommunication between doctors led to unnecessary suffering. However, these negative experiences led Hailey to realize her passion of working in health care. By punctuating her prose with statistics, Hailey further emphasizes how hospitals and health care workers desperately need better communication systems. From here, to subtly demonstrate her qualifications, Hailey outlines her specific goals to simplify information distribution in health care and cites her previous contributions to this area.

Additionally, Hailey humbly acknowledges that she has more to learn in her line of work. Hailey mentions that her company once had to shift clientele from hospitals to smaller, more manageable providers in order to prioritize growth and expresses her desire to gain the expertise necessary to help hospitals. This transitions nicely into her motivations for applying to Harvard Business School while highlighting the specific skills she hopes to gain there. In doing so, Hailey is able to clearly illustrate how an MBA can help her continue to make a positive impact in the world of health care.

—Alison Tan

Cecilia X.

Home State/Country: China
Undergraduate School: Undisclosed
GPA Range: 3.3–3.7
GMAT: 760 T (44V; 50Q)
Work Experience: Investment Banking
Word Count: 1,006

ESSAY

Growing up as an only child surrounded by a close-knit family in Chengdu, China, the extrovert in me drove me to build connections with everything unknown and foreign. Through my adventures, I witnessed and experienced the power of connections firsthand: In middle school, I was the only one brave enough to try talking to the Italian exchange student visiting our school, which earned me a pen pal for life and opened my eyes to Western culture and education for the first time. In high school, chatting up a Dutch couple on a train to Xichang landed me a small role in a bilingual TV production. At 18, talking to an American lady sitting next to me on a flight to Shanghai ended up with me securing a summer job at the Gap. In college, studying abroad at Harvard and responding to an Asian American girl in Cantonese built a lasting friendship and created a unique experience at Boston's Chinatown Afterschool.

This nascent desire to build connections with others, to create similar connections between organizations, and to harness the power of connections only grew as I got older.

At [Company A], connecting with my global colleagues and creating a synergistic team uniquely positioned me to excel in advising cross-border M&A transactions. Working with teammates from [Company A]'s London, New York, Singapore, Lisbon, Sydney and Dubai offices, I built connections with people from different backgrounds by adapting to new environments quickly. I harnessed the power of connections by uniting everyone with a common goal while fully utilizing each member's unique skillset. I created synergies within a team by making sure the sum was greater than its parts.

In 2018 and 2019, we were advising [Company B]'s public tender offer for [Company C], valuing [Company C] at $36.5bn. The client was based in Beijing and Lisbon, the advisors were in Hong Kong, London, New York and Lisbon, while the target had assets across Europe and the Americas. A team of over 40 professionals using three working languages in four time zones with various working styles added to the complexity of the transaction itself and our progress was stalled.

My work stream—offer announcement drafting—required inputs from all parties. Seeing how inefficient the all-party marathon teleconferences could be while not deterred by the fact that I was the most junior member of the team, I reached out to each team's representatives individually to understand their perspectives and address concerns that wouldn't necessarily be shared in a group setting. I was able to incorporate various inputs into a balanced view before hammering out additional details in a large group meeting. This "micro," then "macro" approach I undertook allowed a more productive workflow with fewer conflicts. I clearly articulated the benefits and strategic rationale of the transaction in the final offer announcement in a manner that was attractive to the target shareholders. Combining the small teams into a large cohesive team created a unique capability and the power of this connected team was proven when we announced the largest M&A transaction in [Company A] within ten weeks.

Building connections outside of a strictly business setting and harnessing the power of connections for the greater good is equally important to me, which led to my involvement with [Company D], a Hong Kong health and beauty retail group. One of Hong Kong's biggest social divides is the lack of understanding between locals and expatriates, who make up 10% of the city's population. Recent social unrest further alienated the two groups. In 2018, I saw an opportunity to forge connections between my expat colleagues and native Hong Kong residents. I arranged for [Company A] to become a corporate sponsor of [Company D]'s annual elderly visits. After working with our internal stakeholders from department heads to HR partners, I encouraged over 100 of my colleagues, many being expats, to visit more than 350 elderly Hong Kong citizens. Given the overwhelmingly positive response, this became a tradition in subsequent years. What was truly meaningful to me was how my actions created overlaps between the locals and the expats, which encouraged mutual understanding and built deeper social connections. The power of connections and the social synergies created here not only warmed the hearts of many singleton elderlies in Hong Kong, but inspired a conversation at [Company A] about what we could do to help the local population in times of need.

From there on, I chose to focus on maximizing the power of connections by connecting businesses and creating synergies through M&A partnerships.

By designing a creative joint-venture structure with distribution rebates and a multi-tranche payment schedule, I made the connection between two Hong Kong conglomerates possible. Seeing my client's product—"[Client's Name]-Imported Premium Beer"—at a

7–Eleven next to Budweiser was vivid proof that the powerful connection enabled a local beer brand to expand into new corners of the world and grow exponentially.

Benchmarking a Chinese consumer staple business against 12 competitors defended the value of the business and facilitated the connection between a global player and a China market leader by bridging the valuation gap. The power of connection was evident in the global player's lowered manufacturing costs and secured distribution channels for new product categories.

I meticulously reviewed commercially sensitive information to allow the appropriate level of information sharing while protecting trade secrets of a U.S.-listed company. This gave it comfort in opening up due diligence to Asian competitors and eventually enabled a transaction that pushed forward industry consolidation and revamped the competitive landscape in the infrastructure space.

I have witnessed the transformative power of building connections and creating synergies, and I am inspired to connect with a diverse student body at HBS to create synergies that will make a difference in the world. Post-HBS, it will be my mission to build agility and resilience into businesses through the power of connections. Through synergistic M&As, I will revive struggling businesses, grow promising start-ups to unicorns and create giants that set industry standards.

ANALYSIS

In her essay, Cecilia bridges her natural inclination to make connections with others with her exceptional ability to do so while solving problems in the professional world. Cecilia begins with a series of instances when being extroverted benefited her throughout her adolescence. In addition to revealing interesting anecdotes, this effective hook sets the foundation for their recounting of how she executed synergetic M&A transactions and partnerships. In this way, Cecilia is able to connect her identity as an extroverted only child with her identity as a strong forger of powerful connections with the potential to help other businesses thrive.

Cecilia talks about three of her achievements both inside and outside the business setting while working for her company. For each, she clearly defines the multifaceted problem and the steps she took to solve it. She makes sure to include the most relevant details and quantify both the conditions and achievements in order to accurately describe the issue and the level of expertise required. Additionally, in each step of solving the problem, she discloses exactly what she did and exactly what results that action produced, especially emphasizing her ability to make impactful connections with others.

To conclude, Cecilia fits her ability to form connections with both companies and people into the context of their place at Harvard Business School and beyond. She explains that it will allow her to connect with HBS students of diverse backgrounds. She then discloses that after her HBS experience she aims to create impacts across different areas, from struggling businesses to promising start-ups. Overall, Cecilia lets her accomplishments speak to her qualifications as an admit to HBS and a pioneer in business. She leaves nothing to the imagination except for what great impact she is to make next.

—Isabelle Guillaume

SIDDHARTH J.

Home State/Country: India
Undergraduate School: Indian Institute of Technology, Delhi
GPA Range: 2.7–3.0
GMAT: 770 T (44V; 51Q)
Work Experience: Government & Financial Services
Word Count: 733

ESSAY

Decisions We Take, Boundaries We Break, Relationships We Make

Last year, I fell in love at first sight. She had big gleaming eyes and would laugh like a child. We started dating in a week, I proposed to her a month later, and in six months, we were married. My parents were praying that we don't take just six months to have a baby! Some of my instinctive decisions, often outside my comfort zone, have led me to the most rewarding experiences of my life.

When I left a capital markets job at [an investment bank] to work for an Indian Member of Parliament (MP), many of my friends thought I was taking an insane risk. I was working at a fraction of the salary to set up his office from scratch. But my gut told me that this could be a unique opportunity to have large-scale impact. In six months, the MP became the Deputy Finance Minister, second in command of the Indian economy, and appointed me as his Chief of Staff. Life changed completely, and all of it had happened because my heart told me to believe in someone.

Dealing with financial products for three years at [the bank] taught me a valuable life lesson—returns come with corresponding risk. And just as investors generate good returns by taking measured risks, we make impact by taking difficult decisions in the face of uncertainty. Over two years ago, I read in the newspapers that the HBS-educated Jayant Sinha had quit his corporate career to work on economic policy and contest parliamentary elections. Inspired and intrigued by how a successful professional could utilize his business acumen to effect better governance, I cold-emailed him and offered help. Within a week, I was in his hometown of Hazaribagh, a poor, rural district in the tribal state of Jharkhand, a region marred by extremism and with abysmal income levels.

This exciting new world was a far cry from my comfortable office. I managed the campaign war-room, from where we ran a low-cost, tech-friendly, and creative campaign. We mobilized our party-workers through a call centre, bypassed conventional media through social media and inexpensive pamphlets, and used analytics and marketing techniques to engage more effectively with the voters. I realized how business skills could be used to solve a political problem. And finally, we managed to get Narendra Modi to Hazaribagh and organized a massive rally for him. Jayant won by a record margin! My decision to break boundaries had moulded me to adapt and thrive in unknown settings. Not only did the Hazaribagh adventure lead me to the Finance Ministry; it also motivated me to help drive pro-poor welfare initiatives, such as universal social security and pharmaceutical crop licensing. The Ministry gave me an insider's perspective on the functioning of a government, along with a chance to work on some major economic reforms, such as recapitalizing state-owned banks, setting up a sovereign wealth fund, and deepening capital markets. However, my biggest learning was that the power of relationships can often surpass the power of position. While decision-making authority can often be beyond our control, relationships can still make things happen. The complex Indian bureaucracy is hierarchical and resistant to outsiders. It was inspiring but also challenging to work with people twice my age at the Ministry. I would often offer my help to senior bureaucrats and build rapport through informal chats. Strong relationships thus built helped me mediate complicated negotiations between diverse stakeholders.

Over time, I have realized that who we become is largely determined by the decisions we take, the boundaries we break, and the relationships we make. Our time at HBS will give us the grit to cross boundaries and face unfamiliar situations. When we discuss case studies in a class, share our perspectives over coffee, or work together in a club, we will sharpen our instincts to make better decisions. My teenage hero Albus Dumbledore told Harry Potter that it is our choices that show what we truly are. And my mentor, Jayant Sinha, often mentions how his HBS experience trained him to make difficult decisions. I am sure that in the next two years, we will help each other in shaping our choices, while forging enduring bonds. When we go back to the world, we will face success and setbacks, satisfaction and sorrow, but this section will always be home. Dear sectionmates, I am excited to begin this life-long journey with you!

ANALYSIS

Siddharth's journey is decidedly powerful and unique. Siddharth's hook begins with a personal anecdote about falling in love at first sight. This serves as an introduction to his recurrent theme of stepping out of his comfort zone and learning to trust himself, leaning into "the decisions we take, the boundaries we break, and the relationships we make."

Siddharth leads his audience on a journey through some of his career's most meaningful milestones, revealing insights gained on the way. From his experiences working in investment banking, managing the campaigns of an Indian Member of Parliament, to becoming the Deputy Finance Minister's Chief of Staff, Siddharth crafts a compelling narrative that draws in his audience and establishes the unique perspective he would bring to Harvard Business School.

Siddharth draws his essay to a close by highlighting the impact of an MBA on skills he would like to continue honing, such as decision-making in the face of uncertainty and risk. Rather than explaining how HBS might impact his career, Siddharth more concretely focuses on how his established skills would develop at HBS.

—Hiewon Ahn

J.S.

Home State/Country: New Jersey, USA
Undergraduate School: Georgetown University
GPA Range: 3.3–3.7
GMAT: 730 T (41V; 48Q)
Work Experience: Private Equity
Word Count: 1,043

ESSAY

Among the landmarks of Philadelphia, Boathouse Row has always been my favorite. In a city known for cheesesteaks, rowdy football fans and a statue commemorating a fictional boxer, these charming old-world clubhouses line the Schuylkill River and illuminate its surface with glimmering lights. As a junior transferring to an all-boys Catholic high school in Philadelphia, joining the rowing team was a way to quickly find friends and a niche for myself in my new surroundings. Between drills on the water, afternoons in the weight room and what felt like a lifetime on the rowing machine, one instruction my coaches would always provide was to "make it look easy." This cliché felt ironic while I rowed until my hands were fully covered with blisters, but has now taken on new meaning for me.

Well before I began to row, learning to play the piano was the first time I felt like a natural at something. A needlessly competitive younger sibling, I tried to practice more than my brother every week so I could pull further ahead. I was encouraged by my family and became more self-motivated, even pretending to be sick as a kid so I could stay home and practice all day. It wasn't until I joined a music improvisation group that I realized technical proficiency was only one piece of the puzzle. Even though I had memorized my scales and could play challenging runs, there were many more aspects to consider when performing with others (nobody wants to listen while you endlessly shred). Through time and experience, I learned to listen intently to my bandmates, showcase my ideas more tastefully, and recognize when to step out of the spotlight to highlight others' creative contributions. My technical foundation was critical, but I improved as a musician by practicing with others and focusing on how I could best contribute to the group.

The habits I developed as a musician proved invaluable as a rower. After transferring schools, I was placed in a non-priority boat with only sophomores. My teammates and I trained together year-round to improve our fitness and sharpen our technique. But just like in improvisation, the technical training alone was not enough—we needed to gel as a team. As the boat's sole upperclassman, I established a rhythm: we would socialize frequently outside practices to create a sense of camaraderie, but as soon as we stepped into the boat we would give our full attention to training. With this newfound level of discipline, we practiced through illness and brutal weather conditions and, in turn, developed a strong sense of commitment to the team. Despite being a boat of almost entirely underclassmen, we medaled at the world's largest high school regatta and all moved into the school's top boat the following year. While my personal contribution was important, our success came from the team's cohesive effort—racing "looked easy" because working well as a group had become second nature.

Rowing showed me the importance of teamwork and culture, but it wasn't until I found a sport that I was truly mediocre at that I fully appreciated the impact I could have as a leader. When I stopped rowing midway through college, I was still hungry for an athletic challenge in a team setting. Despite having spent so much time on the water, I was a pathetic swimmer; naturally I joined Georgetown's triathlon team. To improve upon my doggy paddle, I recruited a friend, who spent months teaching me the proper technique in the pool. I organized weekly swim and cycling practices that became popular with my new teammates. Despite my efforts, I remained a poor swimmer and one of the slowest members of the team. However, apparently my stubborn determination and positive attitude had been infectious, and I was elected team captain. As captain, I made the team less intimidating for prospective members by balancing our training schedule to appeal to all skill levels rather than catering to our most talented athletes. I learned that even in situations where I am not particularly skilled, I am able to have a deep impact on the character and growth of an organization.

My extracurricular experiences have served as excellent preparation for my professional career. I understood the value of a strong technical foundation and, because I was not a finance major, worked to master the relevant concepts late at night and often under extreme pressure (I once spent a full night preparing an analysis while passing a kidney stone). But I also learned from improvisation that my technical contribution is only the baseline. While at first it felt uncomfortable, I've made a conscious effort to share my views in group discussions and have grown to contribute significantly to the discourse of team meetings. As I've set the pace for my own development and solidified my role in the group, I haven't forgotten the impact that inspiring positive culture can have on motivating the team. By collaborating enthusiastically, remaining open to others' viewpoints and asking for help often, I encourage my colleagues to do the same. Whether it's been coaching my associate through a complex and time-sensitive analysis or working directly with a CFO through his first refinancing, the people I work with are comfortable coming to me with questions because of the tone I set. As evidence, the firm has recently formalized my leadership role by creating a new title and position for me that previously did not exist. Along with my title change, my job now formally includes a role that previously was implicit: to train and develop the associates who will follow me, including my former mentee, whom I recruited to join our firm.

My perspective on leadership has dramatically evolved. While I still recognize the fundamental importance of technical knowledge, I realize now that fostering group cohesion through effective management is ultimately what makes teamwork "look easy." Leadership can't be practiced independently—HBS is my ideal learning community and sparring ground. I want to live through the successes and failures of the case protagonists and to have my peers challenge my perspectives. Through the Harvard experience, I hope to come away asking better questions and to build a framework for uncertainty that will further define my own brand as a leader.

ANALYSIS

Central to this personal statement is J's distinguished leadership and teamwork and his realization that although technical ability is important, teamwork is what ultimately matters most. From the very start, J vividly brings us into his world and sets the stage for the narrative to be told. Introduced in the first paragraph, the coach's quote to "make it look easy" leads us into the rest of the essay as the reader gains meaning and insight into what this quote means to J.

Not only does J exemplify his leadership and teamwork, but he also illustrates his commitment, dedication, high level of motivation, willingness to work hard, and ability to thrive despite challenges through several anecdotes in the essay, such as practicing piano, joining the triathlon team, and spending a night working while passing a kidney stone.

The key to his essay is the fact that these numerous positive character traits can all be inferred through the story and the various anecdotes that J tells. He paints himself as someone the team can always look to and depend on, but he never states so explicitly.

In the concluding paragraph of the essay, he smoothly ties the narrative together, bringing the quote "make it look easy" full circle and establishing deeper meaning to this quote. He makes clear his objective of obtaining an MBA at Harvard Business School: to practice leadership, something he cannot do independently, by learning through peers and engaging within the Harvard community and experience.

—Leo Shao

II
TURNING ADVERSITY
INTO OPPORTUNITY

Consuelo M.

Home State/Country: New Jersey, USA
Undergraduate School: University of Michigan
GPA Range: 3.3–3.7
GMAT: 710 T (41V; 47Q)
Work Experience: Technology
Word Count: 914

ESSAY

I want you to know that above all else, I am a fighter.

In second grade, the fighter almost came out. One day after ballet, I accompanied my father to pick up my older brother from Tae Kwon Do. I laugh a little thinking back to the situation: me, a little Shirley Temple look-alike, dressed in the pink ballet leotard and tutu that I despised so much, looking on with admiration as my brother chopped his hands through thin planks of pinewood. I turned to my dad and let him know, full of confidence, that THIS is what I was meant to do. I'd be a Tae Kwon Do master.

He agreed that I'd be a natural, but quickly followed up with the honest truth: if I signed up for martial arts, I'd become better than my older brother, and he'd quit the only athletic activity my dad could talk him into attempting. I was frustrated and confused, but more than anything, resigned. I didn't know how to fight for what I wanted, or that I even had that choice. Off to ballet, I went . . .

Since college, I've been developing my inner fighter. It started in the most traditional sense when I joined my university's boxing team a few weeks into freshman year. I usually tell people that I joined to make friends or stave off the "freshman 15" (to no avail), but I think it was really the second grader in me ready for her second chance.

I fell in love with boxing because it helped me find my focus. I learned to clear my head, fully and completely, and drive with full force toward a singular goal. In martial arts, focus is everything. Imagine being in a boxing match and letting your mind wander for just a second . . . Well, that is the same second a fist comes flying toward you. A year of learning that lesson the hard way has stuck with me. Some people turn to yoga or meditation to find their focus; I got there with boxing gloves and a 90-pound heavy bag.

Intense focus and determination are what allow me to fight for what I believe in. In the same week that I joined the boxing team, I also joined SHPE, the Society of Hispanic Professional Engineers. Through SHPE and similar organizations, I fight for the little girls who dream of being scientists or engineers, but whose fathers spend more time encouraging their sons instead of their daughters. I fight for the little boys who are encouraged to focus more on athletics than academics because the basketball court is the only place they see people like them succeeding. Boxing taught me how to fight, but my own experiences and the stories of those around me taught me what to fight for.

A few years after graduation, I began training Brazilian Jiu-Jitsu, an art form that, most importantly, taught me to be fearless. The goal of a Jiu-Jitsu match is to win by submission, which is typically done by putting your opponent into a chokehold or limb lock until they give up. While the idea is that a smaller person (i.e., me, at a lofty 5′2″) can beat a larger, stronger one, let's just say I'm still working on proving that point. More often than not, despite my best efforts, my neck ends up slowly but surely crushed by someone's bare hands. Yet I keep going back.

I love Jiu-Jitsu because each loss teaches me something new about myself and highlights the next goal I get to work toward. Through Jiu-Jitsu I have built the courage to go after every challenge, even when the odds are stacked against me, because no matter what, I come out better for it. At the gym, I've sparred with black belts, professional MMA fighters, and heavyweights. At work, I've pursued positions, projects, and responsibilities that put me head-to-head with Vice Presidents, General Managers, and even our CIO. I am consistently the smallest person on the Jiu-Jitsu mat and the youngest person in the boardroom. But I rise to every challenge because Jiu-Jitsu has made me comfortable being the underdog. I am fearless because I know that with the right strategy, I can persevere. And even when I lose, I learn something new.

Focus, purpose, and fearlessness are things that make a good fighter great. Boxing helped me find the focus needed to keep pushing forward and fighting for what I want, while my involvement with SHPE helped me find a purpose for that energy. Jiu-Jitsu taught me to be fearless in the face of a challenge but recognize the value in defeat. I go after my goals with determination and drive because I can picture the last few seconds in a boxing match and press on, no matter the odds.

I'm coming to business school to continue fighting. Fighting for what I believe in, like promoting diversity and inclusion across all levels of an organization and fighting to make the world a better place through the power of innovation and emerging technology. HBS is the training camp that I need to not only transform into a stronger leader but also a more strategic one, who can see the punches coming before they attempt to land and react appropriately. Over the next two years, through the wins and losses, I want to learn from the best fighters in the world. When the bell rings, and the round begins, I want HBS in my corner.

ANALYSIS

Consuelo begins her essay with a straight-to-the-point hook: she is "a fighter." However, she admits that this label has not always come easy to her, citing a childhood anecdote about how her hesitation to fight for her goals left her stuck with ballet instead of Tae Kwon Do. Many years later, Consuelo got her shot at redemption when she joined her college boxing team. Expounding on her time there, Consuelo reveals that the experience built up not only her physical strength but her emotional resilience as well.

It was precisely this emotional strength that led Consuelo to participate in organizations advocating diverse opportunities for all youths. As influenced by her previous anecdote, Consuelo believes that no child should have their prospects limited because of their gender, illustrating her strong desire for social change. Additionally, Consuelo faced more personal challenges, like mastering Jiu-Jitsu. Though these challenges were difficult, Consuelo's determination to continue with the martial art emphasizes her unwavering tenacity. By explaining how her fighter's spirit has guided her in various endeavors, Consuelo demonstrates that she is more than capable of handling Harvard Business School.

—Alison Tan

Tex I.

Home State/Country: Ohio, USA
Undergraduate School: The United States Military Academy at West Point
GPA Range: 3.7–4.0
GRE: 331 T (170V; 161Q)
Work Experience: U.S. Army
Word Count: 1,026

ESSAY

I was nine years old when my mom first took out a 117% interest loan so that I could have better opportunities than she did. She was born one of eight children in tiny Hopewell, Ohio. She fled her abusive boyfriend at age 20 with a high school diploma in one hand and my infant sister in the other. When she sent me to private school, she was a single mother balancing a toxic job with me and [my sister], who was hoping to be the first in the family to graduate college. I am truly grateful for my mom's sacrifices, and I have continuously sought out challenges to capitalize on the opportunities she wasn't privileged to have. The HBS MBA will help me grow from a military leader into a finance leader, enabling me to help hard-working people like my mom build long-term wealth by increasing their financial literacy and stock market participation through innovative work in the wealth management industry.

When the time came for me to attend college, I knew that my mom could barely manage the rent, so college tuition was out of the question. Luckily, I heard about West Point from a few teachers—a top-ranked education combined with the most intense military training money could buy? It sounded like exactly the challenge I was looking for, and it was free! The discipline and grit that got me through West Point and the collaborative leadership skills that I have refined as an Army combat-arms officer will enable me to thrive at HBS and to help others flourish.

After graduating from West Point, I got on a plane and flew directly to Tel Aviv to begin my Fulbright Scholarship studies. As it was the height of the 2014 Israel-Gaza conflict, I gained invaluable perspective on how others think of themselves and their place in the world while I sheltered from the near-constant rocket attacks. I also developed relationships and made a deliberate effort to evaluate my assumptions and values, which helped me to become a more humble, empathetic, and self-aware person. When I arrived in Jerusalem, I found more than a rigorous master's curriculum. I found the perfect time and place for self-reflection and growth.

While contemplating my future, I discovered that while finance and investing come naturally to me, most people do not understand their options. Why? Only 17 states (34%) require high school students to take a personal finance course. Uninformed citizens fail to realize the full potential of the American economy and the financial markets. If my mom had better guidance on her finances and investing, then perhaps she could have built a future instead of living paycheck to paycheck. I realized that if I could help educate people like my mom and give them the right tools, maybe, just maybe, they could build long-term wealth by wisely investing in the incredible economy that they power. My goal is to help people reach the financial independence that allows them to pursue their passions, take risks, and in the process change the world for the better. I had found my purpose in Jerusalem and now I want to pursue it at HBS.

After leaving Israel, I immersed myself in my role as an Army officer and tank commander, but I did not forget my purpose. In my Army career I have made mistakes and experienced professional adversity. These failures caused me to become a more creative, authentic leader. My most impactful experience, however, has been volunteering with diverse Army families to develop and refine their personal finance and investing plans, leading them toward financial independence. I found that soldiers, much like my mom, have personal discipline and a steady income, but lack the information and tools to save, invest, and build wealth. I believe that building a career in wealth management will empower me to begin transforming the way all Americans approach wealth and prosperity, especially under-served veterans. HBS is the best place for me to begin.

The HBS MBA is the best fit for me because my life and leadership experiences have taught me the importance of truth, excellence, and lifelong learning. I am happiest when collaborating with other members of an intelligent and self-aware learning community who seek to bring out the professional, intellectual, and moral best in one another. I will actively participate in the Finance Club and the Armed Forces Alumni Association, but I am most excited about learning with and from my section mates through the HBS case method. I will contribute my humbling global experience and the leadership skills I developed while building teams in the Army to help them become more agile and decisive business leaders. Their skills and experience will help me grow into a finance leader who enables more Americans to build long-term wealth by increasing financial literacy and equity ownership.

The MBA program's first year Finance and Strategy courses will help me build a strong business foundation as I transition from Army officer to finance professional. I will then aim to complete a summer wealth management associate internship to gain financial industry experience. In my second year at HBS, courses like Strategy and Technology and Entrepreneurial Finance will give me a leading intellectual edge as I begin my business journey. I also hope to return to Israel for the Immersive Field Course in Start-ups and Venture Capital. My work at HBS will complement my military experience and enable me to develop into a knowledgeable, yet perpetually curious and forward-looking finance leader who creates real value.

I want to enable individuals, such as my mom, to make the most of their hard work and to truly benefit themselves, their families, and their communities. I am passionate about helping people build long-term wealth by making well-informed, disciplined investments in the financial markets. Ultimately, I hope that my HBS experience will give me the skills and financial foundation to educate and guide people while leading an online, fiduciary wealth management firm. By doing so, I will reduce financial illiteracy and help prepare Americans for the future. Earning an MBA at HBS will be the best imaginable start to my lifelong business journey.

ANALYSIS

Tex fuses a moving personal narrative with clear purpose in his essay. He opens his introduction with a specific anecdote about his mother taking out a high-interest loan so her children could have access to the opportunities she did not. Not only does this provide insight into Tex as a person and the motivation behind his work, but it also serves as an effective thread throughout his essay.

In the body of the essay, Tex strengthens his theme of using opportunities to his full potential and seeking growth in both success and challenge. By expanding on his journey—graduating from West Point, working on his master's curriculum amidst conflict in

Jerusalem, and leading as an Army officer—Tex effectively showcases his development both as military leader and student. Through making connections with his mother's past to what he observed in his time at West Point and in Jerusalem, Tex seamlessly transitions into delivering his purpose: to help hardworking people and their communities approach wealth and finance differently and benefit from the economy they contribute to.

Tex closes off by homing in on how his time at Harvard Business School will help him achieve his goals and gain further experience as a business leader. Referring to his experience as a military leader, Tex outlines the qualities he would bring to amplify his section mates' learning and the knowledge he would gain from them.

—Hiewon Ahn

TAYLOR B.

Home State/Country: Florida, USA
Undergraduate School: University of Florida
GPA Range: 3.7–4.0
GRE: 332 T (169V; 163Q)
Work Experience: Consulting, Information Technology
Word Count: 1,756

ESSAY

"You're garbage." Those were the last words my mother said to me the day before her overdose on May 10th, 2011. She was responding to my refusal to give her money for opioid pills, her drug of choice. My refusal was in vain, as there was still a final stash she took that night. I struggled through that devastating experience and many similar events throughout my childhood. That pain is what turned me into the person I am today. A person with the perseverance, resilience, and initiative to succeed regardless of the circumstances.

My tribulations with family life did not start or end with my mother's overdose. She struggled with drugs for as long as I could remember. From coming home to an empty house most days to dealing with her erratic behavior while high when she was around, I learned to take care of myself from a young age. My father's unstable and unwelcoming living circumstances meant I could not go to his home instead. The few bright spots in my childhood were the days when he visited me. My father and I would go "window-shopping" to stores as mundane as Target and as extravagant as FAO Schwarz. I loved to see the new toys and electronics on the shelves. On the rare occasions when my dad purchased something new for me, I felt overjoyed bringing it home.

Outside of those excursions with my father, my mother's drug-influenced behavior became more and more dangerous as I grew up. When I was 14, she accidentally set fire to our trailer, and I finally made the decision to leave her home for my own safety. For the rest of the academic year, I organized rotating stays between motels, weekends at friends', and some relatives' couches. I stayed at school doing homework until they locked the gates every evening, and then rode the bus up to two hours to wherever I stayed that night. The world around me felt unstable and insecure. I feared I'd end up back with my mother, but pushed those feelings down to survive through each day. By the next school year, my father moved into his own apartment and I joined him in a stable home. I learned through those months how to have the resilience to survive and thrive no matter the circumstances and how to persevere even when no one offered assistance.

My journey to complete my education was hindered again during college. In my sophomore year, my father suffered a debilitating stroke. His minimum wage job did not provide health insurance, resulting in extraordinary medical bills. Furthermore, he had to stop working during his recuperation. Due to obligations to their own young families and fiscal irresponsibility, my siblings were unable to support my father. As a result, I took the initiative to support him myself while attending school. I took a night job doing janitorial and security guard work for the university sports facilities. Though this work was back-breaking and menial, I spent my junior year judiciously working to provide financial support to my father, but it felt like it was never enough. If I saved $200 by not buying a textbook, he would need $250 for rent. Many times, neither of us had any money. On every school break and call home my siblings told me to drop out of college and get a full-time job like them. However, their lack of higher education meant they struggled to financially support their own children, let alone contribute to my father's needs. I had fleeting thoughts that graduating was a hopeless goal, but I remained steadfast to complete my education and not repeat their mistakes.

Now that I have achieved a level of success and stability, my struggle as a gay teen of color surviving homelessness inspired me to help youth experiencing the same strife. I support a local nonprofit focused on homeless LGBT+ youth of color. As soon as I learned of this nonprofit while an analyst at [Consulting Firm], I worked to sponsor them during my local office's yearly volunteer day. Each year, I recruited LGBT+ colleagues to donate money and volunteer. I did the same once I transitioned to working at [CPG Company], organizing events for [CPG Company] to donate food to their youth events and housing. I was also selected to work on [Nonprofit]'s scholarship review team, ensuring youth would be eligible for educational assistance in nonprofit, business, or trade-focused professions. When I was experiencing homelessness as a gay youth, I didn't have a dedicated resource ensuring I was safe, housed, and securely on a path to higher education. That is why I am passionate about supporting LGBT+ youth of color programs now to increase their support and opportunities.

Starting my career at [Consulting Firm] brought a reprieve from the issues that had plagued my childhood. It was a chance to apply my resiliency and initiative in the workplace. I flourished in my early career, leading full development teams as an analyst and being selected as one of six for an exclusive four-month training program in [Foreign Country]. Despite my early professional successes, one experience at [Consulting Firm] showed me how to be resilient and take initiative to change my own behavior for the better. Six months into a project where I had been consistently praised for my performance, my relationship status came up naturally in a conversation with senior leadership. I noticed the discomfort immediately. Soon after, I felt awkward and excluded as team dinners happened without me and casual office conversations stopped when I entered a room. Within two weeks, I was asked to leave the project due to "budget concerns," despite new analysts continually joining. I later learned from those same analysts that leadership referred to me with a slur after I left. I never had the courage to speak up to HR or anyone in [Consulting Firm] LGBT+ resource groups. I feared repercussions in my professional network and I felt the almost exclusively white, male members of the resource group wouldn't understand my fears. After I grew more confident in my career security, I realized that being resilient meant I needed to bring my whole self to work without hiding a part of my identity, no matter the consequences.

When I decided to leave [Consulting Firm] three years later, I made sure my LGBT+ involvement was on my resume and asked the HR recruiters about their organization's LGBT+ discrimination policy. Once joining [CPG Company], I saw the LGBT+ resource group was again almost exclusively white and male, and took the initiative to change how it approached diversity. I held recruitment events to welcome individuals of other underrepresented groups, international employees, and allies. I organized an online discussion for [CPG Company] employees to learn about the intersectionality of racial and sexual identities with over 250 global attendees. As a result, the LGBT+ resource group was able to support and listen to the newly diverse membership to create actions and dialogue in response to current racial issues.

My transition to [CPG Company] was also an opportunity to draw upon my resilience in a corporate culture where I thrived and made lasting impacts. A layoff announcement very early in my tenure left my team completely disheartened. They wanted to give up, and just put in the bare minimum. I motivated my team to find new projects and demonstrate their value to the organization through successes. My mission was to demonstrate to leadership the essential need for my team. I also led by example, individually bringing an entire department onto a new technology platform that had been suffering from abysmal user adoption rates. As a result of our hard work there were no layoffs on my team, and months later we were recognized as first runner-up for a Global [CPG Company] award due to the results of one of the projects I initiated.

Now, I've reached a point in my career when I want to pursue an area that has always been a passion: consumer products marketing and brand management. Those afternoons window-shopping with my father as a child inspired me to bring those same small joys to others through my career. My career choices have brought me closer to this passion. In college, I pursued an internship at [Retail Company] as a chance to relive those warm memories of childhood. While there, I felt energized learning about the intense data analysis that decides what makes it to the shelf. I went home, excitedly sharing the tricks of the trade with my family, who always viewed [Retail Company] as too expensive compared to our normal shopping at Walmart and Goodwill. After college, I joined technology consulting with a mission to innovate the technology in retail and consumer products.

My recent position supporting marketing technology at [CPG Company] brought me closer to working directly in consumer products. I've gotten the chance to indirectly work in the marketing field, managing innovative consumer digital marketing technology projects. Now, I want to be directly involved in bringing the joy I felt as a child to people through product creation and marketing. While many of my IT, consulting, and product management skills are directly transferable to marketing, the core marketing and leadership skills I need to succeed in that field will come from my experiences in the HBS MBA program.

My values of perseverance, resilience, and initiative will help me succeed in the HBS MBA program and beyond. My multifaceted background will bring diverse perspectives and experiences to classroom discussions and FIELD projects. After conversations with 2020 HBS PRIDE co-president Natalia Ortega, I would continue her work to increase the diversity and international participation within HBS PRIDE. Thinking beyond my MBA and about my long-term goals, my background and professional experience gives me a distinctive perspective to change marketing in consumer products. I plan to incorporate LGBT+ and low-income demographics into product development and marketing decisions, without falling into the currently common pitfalls of patronizing those communities. I recognize this as a missed opportunity within the [CPG Company] marketing teams now, which do not have any projects or teams focusing on those groups. Long-term, my technical background enhances my ability to lead consumer products companies in adapting new technologies for digital marketing. I will lead consumer products marketing to be resilient to changes in marketing methods, technologies, and consumer tastes. The HBS MBA program will help me further strengthen my leadership skills, enabling me to leverage my ability to take initiative, be resilient, and persevere in consumer products marketing.

ANALYSIS

Taylor's journey of perseverance, resilience, and the urge to give back is effectively communicated to admissions officers in their essay.

Right from the hook, Taylor is not afraid to share a raw, personal memory, setting the open and determined tone they use through the rest of their narrative. Instead of dwelling on the hardships of their past, Taylor does an excellent job showcasing their mindset as a learner and person—one with initiative and strength that seeks to grow from the challenges thrown in their path.

Taylor further elaborates on their stance in the body of the essay. In this segment, they expand on their journey and the various successes and challenges that they met on the way. It is also here where they allude to the happier memories of their childhood—going window-shopping with their father—which serve as an effective motif bringing together the narrative of their past as well as their ambitions for the future.

In their final paragraphs, Taylor turns to their experience as a gay person of color and being discriminated against at work due to their identity. Once again, Taylor demonstrates their resilient mindset, relating that this setback became a turning point for them to seek success in their career, not at the expense of their identity, but to empower and give back to those similar to them. This, coupled with their closing remarks on how an MBA will help them achieve their goals, makes for a convincing narrative that demonstrates Taylor's fit for Harvard Business School.

—Hiewon Ahn

Shashanka R.

Home State/Country: India
Undergraduate School: Indian Institute of Technology, Madras
GPA Range: 3.7–4.0
GRE: 740 T (40V; 50Q)
Work Experience: Nonprofit
Word Count: 1,170

ESSAY

The alarm went off at 7 A.M. It was a Sunday and most of the neighbourhood was still asleep. But my mother and I were wide awake. The moment we were eagerly waiting for had finally arrived. My college entrance exam results were going to be announced. Our otherwise lazy Sunday had gone into overdrive as we rushed to the nearby internet cafe to check the results. As I keyed in my details, I heard my mother whisper her prayers under her breath. Within seconds, we were both jumping with joy. My admission was confirmed. And a tiny part of history had been scripted as I became the first student from my village to be accepted into a premier institute.

To me, unlike many others, this admission wasn't as much about my efforts to clear a competitive exam as it was about fulfilling my mother's dreams. It was about seeing her face beam with pride as she realised that years of sacrifice had finally paid off. My father had passed away in a road accident a few months before I was born. Since then, the mantle of the house rested on my mother.

We lived in [a village in South Asia]. Life wasn't a joy ride as my mother worked tirelessly to make ends meet. Whether it was learning the ropes of a bank job or eating one less meal a day, she did everything to give my sister and me a better shot at life. Determined to send us to a reputed local school, she saved every penny by working multiple odd jobs, looking past her own difficulties. The gamut of these sacrifices is what paved the way for many opportunities that helped me grow.

Today, when I look back, we've come a long way. From seeing my mother deny herself new clothes for [a Hindu festival] to being able to buy her a new saree from my first salary—life has come a full circle. I was blessed to have access to the right opportunities because of my mother's farsightedness. And I realised that I wanted to be a similar force in the lives of others like me.

I began by taking up a teacher-in-residence job offered by [a local nonprofit organization] during my junior year in college. I was tutoring high-achieving students from small villages for competitive exams. I vividly remember my encounter with one of my mentees. He was struggling to cope with the academic pressure as he had enrolled late for the program. He was visibly worried and explained to me that his father was a bus driver and he had three younger siblings to look after. He couldn't afford to fail. It was disheartening to see how at the tender age of 15, he carried the weight of his family. While he had immense potential, he seemed to have lost confidence. I was determined to improve his morale and help him succeed. I, therefore, spent time after regular class hours to help him catch up with the syllabus and continued to mentor him even after the program ended. A few years ago, he was accepted at a reputed engineering college. Seeing him achieve this milestone was a great feeling. His success kindled the urge to do more. I wanted to touch more lives by building a community that enables others to realise their dreams.

The first step towards taking the big leap was to strengthen my own skill set and this began when I landed a job at [Global Consulting Firm]. There was no better place for me to learn business and organisational skills than in a leading multinational company. It was an enriching learning experience as I interacted with the top brass of the business world, worked with talented colleagues and learnt the fundamentals of business building. After my stint as a management consultant, I wanted to take the next step towards pursuing my passion.

My quest led me to join [Nonprofit] in [South African city]. Working here has served as an eye-opener as I gained valuable insights into the different aspects of running an educational institution. From admissions to academics to early careers, my exposure to the various departments helped me understand not just the roles and functions of each division but also the importance of a holistic approach to education. At [the nonprofit], I was tasked with solving complex problems we faced as a growing organization. This included using my expertise to create data analytic tools that helped us efficiently target students from diverse socio-economic backgrounds and implementing an integrated student information/data system that fosters improved learning and teaching on campus. I also supported departments such as university guidance to help students explore new avenues for affordable higher education options. I observed the success of [the nonprofit]'s model in our alumni who are now building institutions, running for office and leading change in their communities.

This inspired me to start a similar initiative in my country, back home. Started in December in 2018, [the initiative] was founded with the objective to develop leaders, innovators and entrepreneurs in [South Asian country]. I began by planning camps and pilots and raised funds for this purpose from friends and colleagues. I also recruited five educators, including local entrepreneurs in [South Asian country], for the pilots, the first of which was conducted at my high school alma mater. With the help of [the nonprofit]'s faculty members and mentors back home, I designed a comprehensive leadership curriculum for these sessions. The programs were well received and the host school offered us a yearly contract to incorporate it into their curriculums. The success of these pilots has motivated me to take [the initiative] to other demographics in the future.

Over the last few months, I have worked towards developing the initiative as a platform that empowers young minds and provides them access to various opportunities. It is heart-warming to see an idea that evolved over time come to fruition. In retrospect, it is akin to a puzzle whose various pieces have gradually and beautifully come together—starting with mentoring students in college to tackling business problems in consulting, setting up systems at my nonprofit, to finally founding [the initiative], my own educational community.

I believe that my admission into HBS is the last piece of this puzzle that will complete the picture. HBS's Social Enterprise Initiative (SEI) will equip me with the tools and qualities essential to run my own nonprofit enterprise. It will also serve as a space to collaborate and engage with the experienced faculty members and strong alumni network of the college. Lastly, my education in HBS won't merely be a stepping stone to my success but a means for me to help countless others in their journey to the top. It'll be that opportunity that'll help me act as the catalyst that turns their dreams into realities, just like my mother turned mine.

ANALYSIS

Shashanka begins their essay with a hook illustrating the morning they learned of their admission into a premier institution. In addition to serving as an engaging method to craft the narrative, this allows Shashanka to seamlessly transition into talking about their mother and the origins of the motivation behind their work.

Shashanka homes in on this theme by describing how they have worked towards making it a reality throughout the middle of the essay. From helping a discouraged student from their village realize his potential, to starting an initiative "to develop leaders, innovators and entrepreneurs" in their home country, Shashanka does a great job of specifying exactly what they did to succeed in both learning professional skills and furthering their goal of making a difference in people's lives.

Just as Shashanka relays in the essay, each idea builds upon the other until we have a complete picture of how Shashanka will belong at Harvard Business School. Shashanka explains that they plan to take advantage of HBS's SEI program and use these experiences to catalyze the future successes of others.

—Isabelle Guillaume

Samuel W.

Home State/Country: Texas, USA
Undergraduate School: Undisclosed
GPA Range: 3.7–4.0
GMAT: 710 T (40V; 48Q)
Work Experience: Consulting
Word Count: 1,109

ESSAY

When I was eight, my oldest brother went to prison for armed robbery of a vehicle as part of a gang on the South Side of Chicago. My family had experienced a lot during our time in Chicago, but that was the straw that broke the camel's back—pushing my parents to move our family in search of a community that would offer their six black boys a better life. My family packed up what little we had and moved away from the familiarity of family and friends to Georgia.

Even as a young boy, I was able to recognize the immediate difference in my community. We had moved from a majority black, low-income city to a majority white city with deep southern roots. On the surface, my transition seemed seamless, but on the inside, I was conflicted. I felt like a misfit stuck between two very different communities. And because I had two communities, it felt like I didn't have any at all. At least none that I could call my own.

Over the next decade, my parents pushed my brothers and me hard to make sure we didn't follow the path our older brother took. By the end of high school, I was in the top five percent of my class, had one of the best 800-meter track times in the country, and was on my way to becoming the first college graduate in my family.

But no matter how hard I worked, I still felt like a misfit. In an effort to fit in, I got involved with the wrong crowd. I started drinking and doing drugs. Then one day, things took a turn for the worst. I was pulled over and searched by a police officer. He found the drugs I had with me. I remember thinking, "My life is over." Only it wasn't. As the officer held the drugs in his hand, he looked me straight in the eyes and said, "Trust me, you don't want to go this way. Get off this stuff before it ruins your life. Now get out of here."

That moment was a major wake-up call, and I realized that I needed to make immediate changes in my life.

Two months later I met the Latter-day Saint missionaries. I could see myself in them—they were young and awkward and seemed like they didn't quite fit in. However, they had one major difference from me. They were driven by a strong purpose, and I wanted what they had. I decided to take a step in the right direction and was baptized into the Church of Jesus Christ of Latter-day Saints.

One year later I was serving a volunteer mission in Manchester, England. For two years I sought to help others find what I had found—a sense of community matched with a strong purpose. This consistent period of service helped me come to the realization that helping others find community and purpose was what mattered most to me, and that that belief would be my "North Star" for the remainder of my life.

Upon returning home from my mission, however, the pressures and demands of life hit me with full force, and I once again became consumed with my own goals. Within a few years, I had become one of the fastest 800-meter runners in NCAA history and had taken home an international gold medal while representing Team USA. I had signed a professional contract, had set the World Record in the Road 800-meter race, and had won the bronze medal at the USA Indoor Championships with one of the fastest 600-meter times of all time. Yet, I felt empty and unhappy.

It was then that I, for the second time in my life, learned what mattered most to me. Only this time, I also learned why. This time, I was able to recognize how much help I had been given in my life. My parents helped me by moving in search of a better community. The police officer helped me by giving me a second chance. The missionaries helped me by teaching me the importance of purpose. My coaches and professors helped me by encouraging me to shoot for the stars. I suddenly realized that my hard work and determination didn't make me who I was—my community did.

That moment of realization and reflection was powerful. So powerful, in fact, that I quit track and field that day to pursue opportunities that would allow me to be a more influential mentor. It wasn't just about helping others find community and purpose; it was about walking the path with them. I had been given just that, and I felt a responsibility to give back. Since retiring as a professional runner, I have sought opportunities that will mold me into an influential mentor.

On this quest, I decided to join the consulting industry and get involved in social impact cases focused on the black and Hispanic communities. Advising clients on some of the unique challenges these communities face has felt significant, but now I am ready to make an impact in a more hands-on, "on the ground" way. I want to use the search fund model to acquire and operate a small business in a low-income, predominantly black city. In that capacity, I want to leverage the influence the business will give me to bolster the community. Specifically, I want to work with local nonprofits, community organizers, and social workers to set up a network of mentors for youth and young adults who are lacking community.

But in order to do that, I need help. I need to learn how to acquire and operate a small business from experts like [HBS Professor] and [HBS Professor]. I need to understand how to better connect with and learn from others by participating in the case method with the most diverse set of students in academia. I need to find like-minded individuals who are willing to help me form a network of mentors to bolster communities. These are some of the many experiences I need and can gain from Harvard. I have attended multiple HBS information sessions and have spoken to several alumni. These interactions have been starkly different from the interactions with other schools. HBS students aren't going to business school just for a break or to make more money. They are going to business school so that they can gain the skills and network needed to "make a difference in the world."

This is the kind of community I want to learn from and contribute to. Harvard is my number one choice—there is simply no other community like it in the world.

ANALYSIS

In his essay, Samuel provides an overview of his life's most important experiences and argues why Harvard Business School should be his logical next step. Samuel's writing is personal, frank, and engaging, and it blends his impressive accomplishments with his clear reasons for wanting to attend business school. The hook in this essay is the dramatic story of his oldest brother going to prison, which immediately intrigues the reader. After describing his family's move as a transition, Samuel arrives at the central conflict of his essay: "I felt like a misfit stuck between two very different communities."

During the body of the essay, Samuel describes how he worked to find community after his own struggles resulted in the police finding drugs in his car. He mentions his experiences with religion and the social impact cases he worked on for his consulting company. As he speaks about these experiences, Samuel lists his accomplishments in a way that feels natural and connects each anecdote to the central idea of his essay.

At the end of his essay, Samuel compellingly positions Harvard Business School as the resolution to his conflict by describing it as a valuable community to belong to. He details why he wants to attend business school by naming professors and recounting alumni conversations. Samuel concludes nicely with a sentence that connects to the initial conflict: "Harvard is my number one choice—there is simply no other community like it in the world."

—Westby Caspersen

KWAKU K.

Home State/Country: Undisclosed, in West Africa
Undergraduate School: Kwame Nkrumah University of Science and Technology
GPA Range: 3.7–4.0
GRE: 324 T (160V; 164Q)
Work Experience: Private Equity
Word Count: 1,224

ESSAY

One harmattan morning, as I attended to my early morning chores, bubbling with excitement over the fact that it would be my first day of 7th grade, tragedy struck. The joy of new beginnings quickly dissipated as I received news from my mother that my father had passed away earlier that dawn. I was devastated; I had lost my hero. However, my father's death opened doors to new learnings that shaped my journey as a leader in unimaginable ways.

The sudden loss of my father progressively thrust me into a paternal role within my family, wherein I felt entrusted with an enormous amount of responsibility to be a mentor to my three sisters. Within what felt like an instant, my routine transformed from weekend video game tournaments and carefree pick-up soccer sessions with friends to managing household upkeep and supporting my sisters emotionally and academically, all while dealing with my own grief and anxiety. I embraced the new role and deprioritized most of my hobbies to help my sisters eventually secure admissions to competitive high schools and universities, while striving to be a positive role model along the way.

The opportunity to take on such a key leadership role in my family from a young age dramatically improved my ability to connect with people and taught me to lead with empathy, even amidst challenging circumstances. My father's untimely passing also brought on significant complications to our finances. We had to relocate from our 5-bedroom city-center residence to a 2-bedroom apartment in the suburbs where basic amenities like running water and healthcare facilities were hard to come by. We also had to give up luxuries like eating out frequently and buying expensive clothing. As a boy, I lacked the emotional maturity to adapt to these sudden changes and often unfairly blamed our mother for the drastic change in our circumstances. Though it was a difficult experience, I am grateful for it because it helped me to develop the ability to manage change and disruption effectively both as an individual and within a group.

My mother, though saddled with four children, managed our limited resources with grace and fortitude, while providing us with opportunities to succeed in an increasingly competitive world. She made countless sacrifices along the way, including giving up her lifelong dream of completing a PhD program at a top US university to prioritize raising her children. These acts of selflessness provoked a deep sense of responsibility within me that prompted me to rise to the occasion and contribute my part to our family. In doing so, I opted to remain in [African Country] rather than pursue undergraduate studies in the US, despite being one of the two recipients of the President of [African Country] merit scholarship for academic excellence, in order to help raise my sisters. Today, I am proud to say that my sisters are making tremendous strides both professionally and personally and are showing every bit of the grit and passion that our mother imbued in us. [Eldest Sister Name], the eldest, manages Coca-Cola's brands across West Africa, [Middle Sister Name] is an audit senior with a Big 4, and [Youngest Sister Name], the youngest, just joined a Big Pharma company from college as a pharmacist.

Throughout my personal and professional life, I have had to draw on my resilience, empathy, and ability to manage change effectively to lead myself and others. In 2017, my foundations were tested when I was faced with one of the most challenging experiences of my life during my wife's pregnancy with our daughter. The joy and anticipation of welcoming our first addition to the family was clouded with the fear of losing my wife and daughter to the life-threatening complications that my wife developed over the course of her pregnancy. The mental and emotional distress I experienced throughout this period as I constantly witnessed my wife groan and yell in pain, mostly at night, was agonizing. I spent countless sleepless nights in the hospital over the 9-month period, often having to leave for work from the hospital. During this emotionally tumultuous period, I was assigned my most challenging professional task till date: I was tasked by the Central Bank to develop a restructuring solution for a failing indigenous bank, without which the Central Bank would have to revoke the license of the bank and terminate its operations. The prospect of my wife and unborn child's potential mortality coupled with the potential for many of [my country]'s families to lose their sustenance as a result of failure to deliver on my work, at times, felt unbearable. As this was my first restructuring assignment, it added an extra layer of uncertainty as to how to choreograph the complex turnaround. The bank was on the verge of collapse as key executives had resigned, morale was running low among employees, and the remaining demotivated employees lived in fear of becoming jobless. After an initial review, I realized that we would have to develop a novel solution to save the bank. I led my team to carry out a due diligence to ascertain the cause of the bank's ongoing issues while assessing its prospects by developing multiple restructuring scenarios. After numerous work sessions, many of which I managed on the phone from the hospital at my wife's bedside, we presented six possible restructuring solutions, with varying degrees of political, economic, legal, and social implications, to the Central Bank. This experience strengthened my capacity to navigate ambiguity and helped me to better understand the loneliness and psychological distress that at times comes with leadership, and the need to focus on rising to the occasion to achieve the most ambitious of goals even in the face of stark uncertainty and personal suffering.

In that year, my daughter was born unharmed through an emergency procedure, her mother had a clean bill of health, and I was able to lead my team to provide a very well-received solution to the Central Bank that preserved close to 70% of the jobs in the failing bank. I subsequently received a double promotion and was recognized by the firm for exceeding expectations.

As I reflect on the adversities that I faced as a young boy, and the pace at which I was forced to grow up to support those around me, I am convinced that I am at my best when faced with mounting odds and challenged to evolve outside of my comfort zone. Today, Africa is on the brink of a revolution, and as a private equity investor, armed with the willingness and ability to challenge the status quo, as well as a keen sense of duty to the continent of Africa, I believe an MBA from HBS will provide immeasurable personal and professional development opportunities that will empower me to pursue real economic transformation across the continent. I am confident that my resilience, global perspective, and passion for others, coupled with the learning experiences and networks that I will develop at HBS, will position me for success in ideating, developing, and executing sustainable winning strategies within future portfolio companies in Africa that I have the opportunity to work with. With the HBS MBA experience, I will be well positioned to contribute to transforming medium-sized African companies into well-managed industry leaders with the potential to become regional champions.

ANALYSIS

Kwaku begins this powerful essay with a formative moment from his youth: the passing of his father. Even from a young age, Kwaku's decision to forego his own ambitions for the good of his family is clear evidence of his maturity and depth of character. In addition to highlighting his innate leadership qualities, this story also demonstrates Kwaku's growth mindset and progression as a leader. While he recognizes that he lacked the emotional maturity to adapt to many of the changes that were thrust upon him as a boy, Kwaku demonstrates the experience's importance to his development both as an individual and as a team player.

Throughout the essay, Kwaku's care and admiration for his family is also clear. He spends a significant portion of his essay demonstrating his sacrifice and immense care for his sisters and then discussing how proud he is of them for their accomplishments. Kwaku also talks of his mother's selflessness and how she has inspired him to do better and commit to giving back to his family. These details help show what Kwaku is passionate about and what inspires him in both his professional and personal life.

Continuing with the theme of emotional resilience and grit, Kwaku ends his essay with his experience balancing his work at the

Central Bank with his partner's laborious pregnancy. His relentless commitment to both his work and family is clearly apparent, and his ability to navigate the psychological and emotional difficulties of such an intense situation shows his powerful resolve and dedication to achieve. To conclude, Kwaku describes his desire to contribute to economic transformations in his regional context and the specific role a Harvard MBA will play in these long-term goals. In doing so, Kwaku achieves a touching ending by tying his potential contributions to the world with the personal qualities that he explores within his essay.

—Micheal Zhang

Sabrina F.

Home State/Country: Connecticut, USA
Undergraduate School: Massachusetts Institute of Technology
GPA Range: 3.7–4.0
GRE: 334 T (165V; 169Q)
Work Experience: Engineering
Word Count: 1,431

ESSAY

Grace Hopper once said, "A ship in harbor is safe, but that is not what ships are built for."

As a woman in engineering, I tried to channel her sentiment for risk-taking as I strove to find my place as an outsider—many times over—in a homogeneous field. This fight has been a lifelong odyssey.

From a very young age, while other kids were doing the things kids do, I helped support my family by doing odd jobs before and after school. I ultimately became the first generation [in my family] to attend college. I entered the technology world with the intent to use innovation to improve the everyday circumstances of people's lives. But as an employee of a top-tier tech company, I found myself straddling two worlds—a past life that had taught me so much about the real struggles of many, and a current world of opportunity to which too few are exposed. I was frustrated that I had not yet found ways to create that bridge between technology and those outside the gilded tech world. I recently gained a greater sense of clarity, however, when I started accepting my whole self and focused my efforts on building accessible products and experiences for everyone.

Growing up poor had a number of commonalities with building new technology—there were a multitude of complex risks that needed to be managed and solved on a rolling, real-time basis. My earliest memories are of attempting to manage risks fundamental to a decent life: the risk of not eating, not having electricity or hot water, and sometimes not even having a place to live. After school, I helped my single mother clean picturesque houses, and would often fall asleep in the evenings separating silverware while she waited tables with an improbable smile. Surrounded by chaos, time-constrained problem solving was critical and put me in control. I found purpose in creating better realities. Whether it was setting candlelit dinners when the electricity went out, staging military shower contests when we lost hot water, or scavenging our food from local shelters, solving problems provided a safe haven for me and is the skill I credit for giving me this new life. Despite rising above the circumstances of my childhood, in the back of my mind I felt a mute dissonance; the problems of my past world lingered. Certainly, I gravitated towards socially conscious solutions as a student, working on local government campaigns for meaningful candidates, interning in the US Senate and House of Representatives, and being a volunteer mentor.

When I started my career in tech after college, I continued to problem solve, obsessing over ideas that could have far-reaching impacts both within and outside of Silicon Valley. Despite my efforts to improve others' situations, I felt pangs of guilt as I worked and socialized in a homogeneous, privileged community while keenly aware of the deprivation still existing in my parallel world. However, the more products I worked on and the more I interacted with our users, I realized that my constant straddling of two worlds had uniquely positioned me to better relate to their experiences. My upbringing, composed of time constrained, urgent problem solving had conditioned me to feel less hesitation with taking a risk. And I realized that if I was more accepting of risk, who was I to deny taking a risk in just being my whole self? Perhaps that, along with working on meaningful products, would help be a signal for others to feel less hesitation in joining this field. I started working on programs that helped mentor students from underrepresented backgrounds interested in computer science, being an interview coach for their internships and jobs, and helping them navigate the complexity of entering an engineering team. I made it a point to volunteer for as many consumer facing and developer events and programs, learning firsthand how they interacted with the products I worked on and being in awe of how they applied them to their day to day lives. I grew to love the product development process because I understood the value I was adding in responding to real-world needs and being an ally to our users. I became more confident in my background, harnessing my experience collaborating with others not like me from a young age to build consensus and build meaningfully together. I wanted to be my whole self, being a leader capable of speaking to the needs of our users and collaborating with my teammates to dream up solutions while inspiring others who have also felt like an outsider to do the same. From that moment, every time I would go home and be surrounded by my beginnings, I stopped detaching from it and started asking what role I could play to help build practical and accessible solutions to increase access and opportunity. It was only then I felt true purpose and happiness. Safe as I might be in my current position, I know that I am built for more.

Looking ahead, I want to develop technology-driven, revenue-generating solutions that address the pressing but largely unseen needs of impoverished Americans. I aspire to build a company that develops product solutions in two fields closest to my past, health-care and education. HBS provides access to the people, institutions, tools, and growth required to develop the most meaningful solutions in these areas. It will allow me to challenge my assumptions, lead an organization, and build diverse networks outside of Silicon Valley.

My journey in applying to HBS has been a gift that has confirmed Harvard is where I can best equip myself to be a leader and change-maker on a larger scale. It has provided me a deeper understanding of the community with every case I have read, every RC and EC class I have attended, and each working relationship I have developed on campus. At the HBS Women's Prospective Student Day, I had the opportunity to meet a diverse and inspiring community of students and faculty. The HBS Tech Club provided me with a safe forum to deliberate product ideas. The case discussions I sat in on offered an insightful way to collectively problem solve common pitfalls in scaling a business, challenge each other's assumptions in a supportive way, and learn needed frameworks to practice on our own leadership paths.

Through these experiences I have learned that HBS not only provides practical tools; it also instills the capacity to lead transformational changes for global issues that need leaders. It does not view personal and professional growth as a singular journey; it values collective, diverse problem solving, as exemplified in the case method discussions. This ethos has guided my life; it has motivated me to thrive through my entire journey of upward mobility, and this is why the HBS community felt immediately like home to me. Beyond the ethos of the institution, the sheer amount of resources and opportunities on offer at Harvard is thrilling to contemplate. If admitted, I would participate in the entrepreneurial community of the Rock Center to practice the principles of start-up and product management. In order to develop prototypes that speak to real-world needs, I would take a FIELD course in low-income areas to better understand how I can pull the data science methods and insights from [HBS Professor] and [HBS Professor] to inform the most practical product pipelines. I plan to collaborate with my Tech Club peers as beta testers within the i-lab, pushing ideas to full working fruition as I pitch for funding and support in the New Venture Competition. I will harness my knowledge of the Valley to lead WesTrek trips, invite speakers, and be on call to students as we grow together. More broadly, I am confident that the unusual perspectives and specificities of my own lived experience will be enriching to my section and the greater HBS student body. I have grown through difficult decisions and hard processes; my whole life has been filled with case studies of my own.

Having navigated through so much, I am ready to embark on the next set of challenges with a diversity of backgrounds and viewpoints at HBS. In facing this new step in my professional development, I am mindful of [HBS Professor]'s guidance that effective leadership is predicated upon "ownership of your convictions, actions, and impact on others." In my career to date, I have held on to the conviction to pursue the right things; I am certain that an MBA from Harvard can play a pivotal role in making sure that they have the biggest impact possible.

ANALYSIS

In a powerful personal narrative, Sabrina connects her background to the positive impact she plans to make on her community. Her hook is a quotation from Grace Hopper. Referring to the quote, Sabrina indicates that she is a woman in engineering and believes in effective risk-taking. This strong "thesis" signals to the reader that Sabrina intends to elaborate on her experience in engineering and her ability to take risks as she relates to her qualifications for business school.

In the introduction, Sabrina subtly notes her achievements as an employee of a top-tier tech company while also introducing her internal conflict: a struggle "to create that bridge between technology and those outside the gilded tech world." In the body of her essay, Sabrina demonstrates how she reconciles and bridges two socioeconomically different worlds. Through anecdotal evidence, she touches on the origins of her problem-solving ability as well as her work developing meaningful products.

Towards the end of her essay, Sabrina's resolution is that her understanding of poverty as well as product creation within Silicon Valley equips her to create "technology-driven, revenue-generating solutions that address the pressing but largely unseen needs of impoverished Americans."

Sabrina never provides a negative description of her background; instead, she poignantly demonstrates her positive mindset, her ability to take calculated risks, and her aptitude for problem-solving in the face of extreme challenge. Her background explains to admissions officers the larger impact she plans to make with an MBA and a continued career in technology.

—Taia Cheng

EJ.L.

Home State/Country: South Korea
Undergraduate School: Waseda University
GPA Range: 3.7–4.0
GMAT: 750 T (40V; 50Q)
Work Experience: Private Equity, Investment Banking
Word Count: 962

ESSAY

Growing up sick with a rare heart disease and living with a high risk of heart attack to date, I learned at a young age the importance of perseverance in pushing my boundaries. From the age of five, I had to fight against the [heart disease] and many other complications including anemia and asthma, and after six years I was left with the chronic arrhythmia. While enduring through the procedures and having a heart monitor attached around my chest were painful experiences as a child, the most painful memory was being unable to learn and experience things outside of the hospital room. When I finally left the hospital, I made a promise to myself that I would explore the world, keep learning new things that I was once physically unable to.

The first challenge I took on after leaving the hospital was to pursue my long-held interest in being a swimmer. Not surprisingly, it took me the longest time to gain enough stamina to keep up with others as breathing itself was a problem for me with asthma. But after continuous training and breaking through my limits, which I enjoyed every second of, one day I became able to finish fifty meters without stopping, and in my fourth year of swimming I made it to the city's swim team. Such experience not only gave me confidence but also formed my attitude of constantly challenging myself.

Whenever I face a new challenge, whether it is a personal one or a professional one, I take myself back to the early days in the hospital and I become immediately ready to take the next step forward, and to even seek further exciting challenges. Upon joining investment banking at [Investment Bank] in an international office, I took on a challenge to push the cultural boundaries of the firm. Recognizing the domestically enclosed work customs which led my division to repeat similar pitches to different clients, I pushed for more systemic cross-regional information exchanges across the firm, leveraging my unique viewpoint as the only foreigner in a division of seventy. I started by putting together regional deal case studies and leading review sessions with multiple global offices on a regular basis. Colleagues in other offices appreciated opportunities to learn about regional transactions, and in return, they started to proactively share their best practices and market insights, which became a source of inspiration for our team to come up with creative and innovative solutions for the clients. As a tangible outcome from the increased collaboration, our team won a number of large equity transactions including a mega deal mandate, and it was one of the most rewarding experiences to be recognized by senior management for my contribution to the division's success.

In addition to challenging boundaries for the firm, I consistently strive to challenge my own professional capabilities. My endeavors especially paid off when my team was mandated with a cross-border deal. Due to the unique nature of the transaction, our team initially had difficulties coming up with the optimal execution strategy. I pushed myself to step out of the comfort zone, facilitating months of weekly conference calls to discuss the deal structure with the client, teams from other regional offices, and legal counsel. Additionally, I took the lead on drafting the marketing materials to be more specifically catered towards foreign investors, which led to a greater interest in the offering. The successful execution after months of hard work set a precedent for multi-million-dollar cross-border transactions across the franchise, and the client's feedback that I played an integral role despite being an Analyst was extremely rewarding.

Outside of work, using the lessons I learned in pushing my boundaries, I organize events to coach domestic violence victims for job interviews as a means to empower them in pushing beyond their own boundaries. One of my most fruitful experiences was assisting a lady in her fifties who had just left her abusive husband, with no prior work experience. While at first it appeared insurmountable to overcome her hurtful past and present herself again in front of others, after drafting her resume together and looking for workplaces that she would feel comfortable for, I finally saw her break free from the chain of her past when she found a job at a local bakery and sent me her hand-baked Christmas cookies last winter. The letter that she sent along with her cookies saying how she is happily supporting her daughter's college tuition gave me motivation to continue exploring ways to make a positive and tangible impact on others.

For my next challenge, I am looking to expand my professional ability through more cross-border transaction experiences on the investing side with the goal to ultimately become one of the first female leaders in the private equity sector in the country. Fortunately, I will be able to take that first step as a pre-MBA Associate at [Private Equity Firm] led by [HBS Alum], whose main investment focus is cross-border transactions throughout the region. I am fully aware that my dream of pioneering female leadership in private equity will require unrivaled mental fortitude, leading industry expertise, and globally outstanding leadership. To that end, I have no doubt HBS will provide me with the perfect tools to continue to challenge real world problems and make positive impacts on people and businesses, and to grow into a transformational leader. Thanks to the thorny path I walked through in my early life, I am grateful for the ability to challenge and take my life as I would like. The life at HBS is another challenge that I look forward to, and I am ready to make the most out of my two years.

ANALYSIS

In this personal narrative, EJ describes the challenges she faced and how those experiences have inspired her to take action in many facets of her life. EJ shares that her experience growing up with a rare heart disease taught her to push her boundaries through perseverance and continual exploration. This also introduces a theme that centers the rest of the essay.

Throughout the body of her essay, EJ shares anecdotes that establish the consistency of her character. EJ describes how she developed confidence and a challenge-seeking attitude through swimming. EJ also highlights how her unique perspective created an individual impact at the investment bank by pushing the firm's cultural boundaries and earning recognition from senior management. By empowering victims of domestic violence, she also instilled these values in others. Returning to her theme of seeking challenges, EJ asserts that she aims to become one of the first female leaders in private equity. She resolves that her difficult experiences have given her the ability to pursue challenges and that Harvard Business School is another challenge that will push her towards her goals.

Rather than portray her health condition as an unwelcome burden, EJ highlights the role it has played in shaping her attitude of perseverance despite challenges. Through examples demonstrating her ability to break boundaries and create improvements in different facets of her life, EJ shows Harvard Business School admissions officers that she possesses the skills and drive necessary to realize the goals she plans to pursue with an MBA.

—Eric Elliott

Olivia W.

Home State/Country: Nevada, USA
Undergraduate School: Brigham Young University
GPA Range: 3.7–4.0
GMAT: 720 T (44V; 47Q)
Work Experience: Consulting
Word Count: 1,438

ESSAY

Sixty feet up, I swung from Corona Arch in Utah's canyonlands and weighed my options. Midpoint in my descent my long braid caught in the rope and threaded through my rappelling gear. I stopped my downward momentum in time to prevent injury, but my hair was wound and wedged tightly. Climbing up a few feet to create slack, I worked to pull my hair free, but it was impossibly tangled. With limited resources, tethered by only sixty feet of rope, I needed a solution. I called to my canyoneering companions below to pull the rope taut so I could use both hands. Then I swung my small pack off one shoulder and dug through it to find the serrated switchblade intended for cutting rope, not hair.

As a supply chain consultant, I often face challenges that require quick and resourceful response as while climbing Corona. For example, I was assigned to a project where the team I joined was behind schedule. In just four weeks we were expected to present client executives with answers to a long list of complex questions. Like using my rope knife, I confronted the client's needs with assertive resolve, redirecting my team's initial plan. I led us to use advanced analytics tools, personally coaching two team members from Korea and India. My creative approach to our problem accelerated data cleansing and analysis iterations, allowing us to exceed expectations ahead of schedule. Our work resulted in a strong client relationship with requests for additional work proposals worth millions of revenue dollars.

This tenacity and skill for creative problem-solving was developed early in my life. I took a creative educational path, happy to be an autodidact, and graduated from high school at fifteen years old. Not old enough for a driver's license and rather young to go away to college, I rode my bike to work and class at nearby University of Nevada, Las Vegas (UNLV), despite the 110-degree heat. Mom said it built character. I strategically chose credits that transferred a year later to my school of choice: Brigham Young University (BYU).

I was determined to have a foreign experience but lacked funds for a traditional study abroad. I found a nonprofit program to sponsor me as an English teacher in Russia. While there I didn't live in university housing with English-speaking students but instead with a Russian family in a poor, rural area. I spent that invaluable semester teaching English to grade-school children. By refusing to succumb to limitations, I made my dream for international travel a reality.

I was different from peers in college because of my age and in Russia because of my nationality. Through this difference, I learned to appreciate and optimize diversity while asserting my authenticity. For me, authenticity means accepting myself and others, expressing my thoughts honestly and clearly, learning from my mistakes, and taking actions consistent with my values. I work to be authentic.

For example, during my first college internship I was the only female on a fifteen-person team. My job was to establish operations with a newly contracted school district, organizing transportation for special needs students. Despite age and gender, I connected with co-workers and did my job so well that when my employer learned I was too young to rent a car—something they took for granted I could do because they failed to notice my age and something essential to my accomplishing my work—they accommodated me by providing prepaid cards for taxi rides and pairing me with another team member as needed. I proved such an asset to my employer that they offered me a full-time position at the end of my internship, which I declined in favor of returning to BYU. They extended offers over the years. Although I turned these down, I did recommend several friends whom they hired. This experience of being myself even though I was different from the group and even from the employers' expectations reinforced my commitment to authentic representation in every aspect of my life.

While at BYU, my commitment to authenticity helped me cultivate a collaborative dynamic within my supply chain team. We competed at several twenty-four-hour case competitions, which can induce the same anxiety as dangling sixty feet above the ground with my hair caught in a carabiner. Our collaborative culture, centered on open discussion, helped us work under pressure to develop winning solutions. We were awarded first place at the BYU supply chain case competition, first place at the Mountain-West competition, and fourth place at the national level. While at BYU I also served as the supply chain program's Executive VP of External Relations, fostering connections between students and professionals. Harnessing my ability to connect with others I built a network that directly linked three of my classmates to full-time jobs, and many underclassmen to internship offers. My dedication to building collaborative teams and meaningful connections has served me and is a core value of my personal and professional life.

During my three and a half years with [Professional Services

Firm], I've worked on sixteen projects with thirteen different clients, many of whom are global and Fortune 500 companies. In addition to my core client work, I sought opportunities for organized community service upon joining [the firm], which further developed my collaborative skills and power for creative problem-solving. Discovering a nascent pro bono consulting program for local nonprofits, I noticed an upcoming project for a global start-up accelerator based in Boston. [Their] mission to provide equity-free funding to impact-focused start-ups resonated with my values, so I joined [the firm]'s project team.

Unlike carefully structured teams for standard client projects, my pro bono team was a coalition of willing, passionate people donating night and weekend hours. A few weeks in, our project manager became too busy with core client work to continue. Due to my strong relationships with teammates they asked me to fill the leadership role. We had just completed the strategic assessment and I recognized that to deliver real value we needed to provide [the start-up accelerator] something more tangible: they needed a tool to enable their work. My teammates proposed we recommend tools on the market or identify technical requirements for future development. I knew we could do better than simply provide recommendations. Understanding my client's unique challenges, I built an Excel-based tool to automate workflows and visualize data. After several iterations with my team and the client, the tool offered an intuitive user design and custom data dashboards. [The start-up accelerator] received the tool with enthusiasm, then expanded its use to all internal teams. Months later, they reported that the tool helped them secure their largest donation to date.

The project became a hallmark narrative for [Professional Services Firm]'s bourgeoning pro bono consulting program. I formally reported our success on several occasions, including at [the firm]'s quarterly northeast partners' meeting. Interest in my presentations rallied support for the creation of a larger, more formal program which [the firm] coined [Program Name]. I managed our first project during the Boston pilot. [The program] is now in Boston, Chicago, and Seattle—going nation-wide in 2020. My [project] experience proved I can affect positive change. It also validated my desire to exceed creative problem solving by capitalizing on what I call my "maker nature" producing real products that deliver real value.

There is no better vote of confidence in my ability to deliver real value than the recent decision made by [the firm]'s Senior Partners to sponsor me as a Digital Accelerator. This promotion involves a year-long role of weekly protected time intended for training and experimentation with emerging technologies. Additionally, in November I was asked to lead the development of a supply chain analytics platform that will change the way [the firm]'s supply chain teams deliver value to clients. These opportunities are important and exciting to me because I see their potential for me to affect significant positive change.

The case-based learning model and carefully crafted student experiences at HBS are even more exciting to me because they promise exponential opportunity for me to contribute in real ways. I hope to utilize Harvard's Innovation Lab and field courses in operations, technology, and entrepreneurship. While exploring the student experience, my husband and I were drawn to the Partners' Club and community culture at HBS. We believe this will support my efforts to develop relationships with classmates, faculty, and alumni. Earning an MBA at Harvard will be an ongoing adventure as arduous, breathtaking, and awe-inspiring as rock-climbing in Utah's canyonlands. I intend to face academic and professional challenges at HBS with the same tenacity, creativity, and authenticity as I do rappelling because my life depends upon it.

ANALYSIS

Olivia crafts a well-rounded essay, highlighting her career successes and key characteristics while simultaneously giving us a glimpse into her thrilling personal life. Olivia hooks the reader in by setting the scene of a life-changing rock-climbing escapade. The effortless link between her rock-climbing story and work experiences demonstrates her "quick and resourceful" approach is an inherent ability.

In the body of the essay, through retelling experiences, from turning a team around in four weeks to studying abroad in Russia, Olivia shows how she has always refused "to succumb to limitations." Meanwhile, the unique personal details embellishing these retellings, like Olivia riding her bike in scorching heat to school, make the essay more memorable. She finishes narrating each of her experiences by stating how she has developed through them, allowing her to illustrate her many desirable characteristics for Harvard Business School, from authenticity to commitment to healthy collaboration. Furthermore, the successfully intertwined narration of Olivia's clever solutions and pro bono work intelligently shows her creative mind and passion for using her talents for good.

Olivia outlines her natural "fit" to Harvard Business School by giving specific examples of the school's aspects that excite her. Using the rock-climbing story like an extended metaphor, Olivia establishes a personal bond with HBS.

—Ece Hasdemir

III
PROFESSIONAL DEVELOPMENT

Greg H.

Home State/Country: Virginia, USA
Undergraduate School: Rensselaer Polytechnic Institute
GPA Range: 3.3–3.7
GRE: 328 T (161V; 165Q)
Work Experience: Nuclear Engineering, Military
Word Count: 1,036

ESSAY

> "Tenacity, Dick, stay with the [enemy] until he's on the bottom."
> —Dudley "Mush" Morton, Captain of the submarine USS *Wahoo*
> to Richard "Dick" O'Kane, his Executive Officer
> and future Captain of the USS *Tang*

Tenacity is persistence in seeking something valued or desired. Some call it grit. Things will not always go your way, but tenacious people don't give up easily. I was a tenacious kid. At age six I visited the United States Naval Academy in Annapolis, Maryland, and felt something electric in the air. This was somewhere I wanted to be someday. I decided that I would do everything in my power to go to Annapolis, study nuclear engineering, and ultimately serve on an aircraft carrier. The logic seemed straightforward at the time, but plans don't always survive first contact with the enemy. I studied hard. I became an Eagle Scout. In high school, I received the John Philip Sousa Award and a varsity letter for track and field. Despite my best efforts, I was not accepted to the United States Naval Academy. Undeterred, I continued to pursue my dreams of a commission and a degree in nuclear engineering at Rensselaer Polytechnic Institute (RPI) through a Navy ROTC scholarship.

I was dead set on studying abroad in college. German was my favorite subject in high school, and I joined the Navy to see the world. Although no ROTC student at RPI had studied abroad in years, I was determined to find a way. I wanted to study in Germany but was unable to find a feasible option. Instead, I found a viable opportunity near Copenhagen, Denmark. Having earned enough Advanced Placement credits to study abroad without affecting my ROTC scholarship, I set a course, made my plan, and submitted a proposal to my instructors. The six months that I spent in Denmark were among the best I have known. I learned to speak and read Danish from the subtitles on television. I visited 12 countries, learned how to cook, and made lifelong friends. While living overseas life was similar, but also new and different. I loved this feeling and knew I would someday need to feel it again.

During commissioning, I volunteered for submarine duty knowing it would be an incredible challenge. My career started with a rare opportunity to spend six weeks at Navy dive school in Panama City, Florida. Waking every day at 4:30 A.M., we crawled through sand pits, were beaten underwater in pools, led teams of our peers on high-risk training dives, and learned to remain calm even as everything around us went wrong. There were times where I felt like I wouldn't make it, but I was persistent. I wasn't going to give up. I would either leave dive school as a graduate, or on a stretcher. With my body trained, I went on to Naval Nuclear Power school to train my mind. It started with six months of 80-plus-hour weeks studying in a secure building without phones or computers, followed by another six months of 14-hour shifts on an operational reactor plant. By the time I finished, I was a qualified nuclear reactor plant supervisor, but that was just the start. The efforts of the past year would begin anew on a new type of reactor once I reached a submarine.

I was assigned to the USS *Hawaii* stationed in Pearl Harbor, Hawaii. As the first new officer aboard *Hawaii* in over a year, it was difficult finding a mentor. My peers were already fully qualified. They had earned their "dolphins," the badge a submariner wears when they are certified to drive, fight, and save the ship in any imaginable circumstance. I struggled early on. My Navigator pulled me into his stateroom and said, "You're behind on your qualifications. Five hours a day is too much sleep. Make a round turn if you want to be respected here." I didn't like what he said, but I took his feedback and fought on. For the next several weeks I slept only three hours a night and exceeded all expectations regarding my qualifications. I wouldn't make any excuses. I gave my best effort, and by the time *Hawaii* was ready for her 2014 deployment I had my dolphins as well.

During that seven-month deployment, *Hawaii* visited Japan four times. After the first day in Yokosuka, I fell in love. Everything was new again. The same feeling I experienced in Denmark had returned. I bought a Japanese language textbook, and I began to study every day. At sea, I studied underwater by myself in the dark of my stateroom when I otherwise would have been sleeping. The challenge of learning Japanese was my escape, and it helped me define where I wanted to go next. Although I enjoyed Europe, I loved the idea of living in Asia and volunteered for duty on the USS *Ronald Reagan*, a U.S. carrier stationed in Japan. Through a nexus of effort and remarkable serendipity, I had become a naval officer and a nuclear engineer serving on an aircraft carrier living overseas.

Now, after three years in Japan, I have learned and experienced so much, yet I strive for more. Tenacity is part of who I am today and keeps me on course throughout my life. I know that it will continue to help me in the future as I leave the military to pursue an education in business. It will keep me on course as I become the change-maker, problem solver, and cultural bridge-builder that I aspire to be.

Tenacity is the characteristic that kept "Mush" Morton and the crew of the USS *Wahoo* alive through seven Pacific submarine patrols during the Second World War. Rejecting the notion that there was one right answer, "Mush" met his problems head on by shooting torpedoes "down the throat" of enemy ships. That same tenacity earned Dick O'Kane the Congressional Medal of Honor and made the USS *Tang* the most successful American submarine of the Second World War. In my own time spent underwater in service to my nation, I thought often about the grit and persistence of men like "Mush" and "Dick." I realized that I had a measure of tenacity as well.

ANALYSIS

Starting with a quote that alludes to his military background, Greg powerfully introduces his essay by emphasizing the word "tenacity": an attribute he considers central to his identity and one that is mentioned repeatedly throughout the essay. The trait he believes characterizes him the most is his innate drive to overcome hardship and accomplish set goals in the face of adversity, which ultimately results in his admission into the Rensselaer Polytechnic Institute with a Navy ROTC scholarship.

In the body of the essay, the reader is provided with insight into Greg's experiences in the military and living overseas. A second characteristic is introduced in this portion of the essay: Greg's ambition and desire to exceed "all expectations," which drives him to passionately pursue his interest in nuclear engineering.

In short, Greg's story incorporates academia with physical training, connecting what he learned from both areas to a career in business. He concludes the essay by referring back to "tenacity," reminding the admissions office of the essay's central theme of resilience.

—Sophia Klonis

NALIN K.

Home State/Country: India
Undergraduate School: Indian Institute of Technology, Delhi
Grading System: 9.03/10 (Alternate Grading System)
GMAT: 760 T (44V; 50Q)
Work Experience: Consumer Packaging Goods, Start-up
Word Count: 908

ESSAY

I vividly remember the summer of 2009. While still in high school, I installed an accelerometer on my tennis racquet to measure the speed of my forehand. Furthering my passion for tennis with this "smart" racquet, I tracked weekly changes and improved my game. I not only felt proud of my creation but found immense satisfaction in building new things. Captivated by this "invention" and keen to explore "what next" led me to study engineering at IIT Delhi instead of taking the much-advocated path of continuing in my parents' medical profession.

Apart from building technical prowess, IIT Delhi groomed me as a young leader via a multitude of experiences—captaining the hostel tennis team and organizing the institute's annual literary festival. The most formative of these occurred in the summer of 2015. 15 days before the term start date, a long-existing rule of completing 100 hours of service at the National Cadet Corps (NCC) before the final year was brought into strict enforcement. With this, around 200 final year students stared at a potential delay in their graduation by an entire semester. While the larger emotion on campus was of angst and dissatisfaction, as the leader for the 30-member Board for Student Publications (BSP), I chose to engage with a difference and launched an open forum on the BSP website to debate the NCC ruling and invited deans and students to discuss other critical issues. This self-balancing and transparent reverse-feedback mechanism conveyed the voice of reason to administration in an unbiased manner and not only helped relax the NCC ruling but also opened dialogue on various pending issues, such as the need for a Gender Awareness Committee and advocating LGBTQ rights during subsequent Senate meetings. Such results inspired me to lead with purpose and imparted valuable skills in navigating conflicts involving large numbers of people.

I got an opportunity to practice these when, at 23, I was entrusted to turn around the largest personal care manufacturing site in India. The plant produced 40% of India's shampoo sachet demand, but production had declined ~5% every month for the quarter leading to my appointment. Applying my engineering capabilities, I introduced multiple changes to reduce machine breakdown, improve product changeover times, but surprisingly, these even failed to reach the shop-floor because of the rife disagreements amongst my seven-member executive team, the people I had entrusted to drive these changes. One-on-one conversations with each member pointed to the fact that poor production planning by the senior-most member reporting to me was inducing unnecessary chaos. His work style disrupted others' daily schedules and left them with little time for new initiatives. Therefore, I partnered with HR and coached him and when that failed too I fearlessly drove consensus to replace him, who had eight more years of experience than me. Working with the HR team, I found an alternative role for him and honestly communicated the decision. This hard but meaningful decision synergized the team and created a pathway to implement incremental changes such as introducing a data-driven operator incentive scheme that boosted plant productivity phenomenally and we ended the year as the #2 ranked site across our company in South Asia in terms of operational excellence. Here I discovered both the courage and the empathy to drive tough but necessary changes which are the key hallmarks for any business leader.

After 2.5 fulfilling years at our company, when I transitioned to a leading E-Commerce Transport Company, these values were put to a grueling test. As I took charge of the six-membered pricing and strategy team for the Retail Express (RE) business in January 2019, I saw that despite our optimized truck-network planning and utilization, our gross margins were below industry average. Delving into the field, I realized that our pricing platform was too simplistic and was unable to predict prices of the diverse packages we picked from the market, promoting cluster leaders to engage in arbitrage pricing. This intuitive price they quoted was often lower than competitive rates, making about 20% of our business and specifically 16 micro-markets unprofitable to serve. Championing profitability over un-sustainable growth, and defining intervention in unexplored markets that would preserve revenue targets, I convinced the CEO and the board to withdraw from underperforming markets and led efforts to revamp our pricing platform. I travelled six cities in a month, social-ized this differentiated approach with cluster leaders personally, and won their confidence. In Q2 2019, while RE grew only 17% (as com-pared to an earlier demanded 20%), our gross margins improved by a staggering 40%. Today a quarter later, RE continues to grow at 52% CAGR, and the new pricing platform has improved yields (price/kg) 2% every month.

Thus, empowering people with the right tools and percolating a culture change that created a better and sustainable business, I grew many-fold as a leader and team player. Designing and driving change with large teams have characterized my journey so far. I want to build on these further and innovate at the intersection of technology, logistics, and people, to modernize India's logistics industry that today sheds $60B of produced GDP across the value chain. HBS is a cogent next step towards this. Inspired by my college senior's journey at Harvard, I am excited to debate 500+ cases with talented peers, learn from exceptional faculty, ideate with innovators such as [HBS Director] and [HBS Professor], and grow into a leader who can shape the future of India's logistics industry.

ANALYSIS

Beginning with a hook that provides context regarding his background in engineering and demonstrates his sense of creative innovation since high school, Nalin connects his love of building something new to his ability to produce quantified results in an essay that constructs a clear, chronological account of three formative business management experiences.

Throughout the piece, Nalin maintains an appropriate balance between describing the challenges presented by these different situations and reflecting on how each has contributed to his personal growth. Whether through navigating student-administration conflict or resolving company production decline, Nalin consistently displays his initiative and willingness to go the extra mile while integrating relevant statistics to highlight the positive outcomes of his work.

The essay's conclusion expands in scope to reflect on these past experiences as a whole, allowing the reader to come away with an understanding of Nalin as a driven, flexible "leader and team player," with strong interpersonal skills, problem-solving intuition, and the ability to create tangible, effective results. Looking ahead, Nalin outlines how Harvard Business School fits into his future trajectory and his targeted goal of continuing to "innovate at the intersection of technology, logistics, and people," an effective method of defining his purpose to the reader. Overall, the essay reads coherently and holds a defined sense of purpose throughout, blending resume accomplishments and admirable character traits to create a strong picture of a prospective MBA candidate.

—Cynthia Lu

Emma A.

Home State/Country: Connecticut, USA
Undergraduate School: Johns Hopkins University
GPA Range: 3.3–3.7
GMAT: 720 T (42V; 45Q)
Work Experience: Private Equity
Word Count: 1,100

ESSAY

"See those letters up there? They're over six feet tall," she whispered, grinning. Standing below Michelangelo's dome inside St. Peter's at the Vatican, my mother pointed at the lapis-lazuli letters in the mosaic hundreds of feet above us. After confirming the letters' size relative to a man standing on the platform above, their significance was clear, and my passion for art, its geometric precision, and its import in the world had been ignited. While my interest in art history has only grown since that moment 14 years ago, I've also discovered passions for the arts more broadly, business, and the environment. Experiences stemming from these interests have led me to integrate art and analytics, build adaptability, and grow and exercise a passion for positive impact.

Art + Analytics: From Evensong to EBITDA

In addition to an early interest in Renaissance art, studying ballet for 12 years inspired a passion for classical music and, subsequently, a love of singing that continues today. While the formulaic precision of classical music intrigues me, singing is even more captivating to me. From joining a church choir in third grade to completing a European tour with a high school group to taking lessons at the Peabody Institute, singing has allowed me to share arguably-underappreciated genres of music with the community. Most recently, after moving to Texas last summer, I tried out for and joined the adult choir at a local church. I'm very excited to continue my pursuit of music while co-leading our 2020 tour to New York.

While I indulged my passion for singing through voice minor lessons at Johns Hopkins, by studying art history and business courses I further cultivated my interest in art and analytics. Additionally, interviewing a student investment group for a *Johns Hopkins News-Letter* article significantly expanded my opportunity paradigm of the intersection of art and analytics. Just as art history demands a combination of aesthetic appreciation and well-researched logic, finance presented fascinating ways to leverage research in solving business challenges. While proactively moving up the financial knowledge curve helped me secure internships with [Asset Management Firm] and [Investment Firm], recruiting for investment banking roles as an art history student at a "non-target" school posed significant challenges. After countless cold emails and informal conversations, I received and accepted an offer with [Investment Bank] in Milwaukee. Upon arrival, I strove to build a rigorous analytical base while applying the dual art-plus-analytics lens from my humanities background, thereby earning the respect and trust of my originally-skeptical colleagues. Receiving "top bucket" performance ratings and being selected for an Associate promotion felt like affirmations of the value of blending art and business.

A Quest to Become U-Haul's Top Customer

Transitioning from art to investment banking represented one big leap—studying in Italy and moving to four different cities in the span of four years helped me further appreciate the importance of adaptability. While I'd studied Italian at Hopkins, living with a host mom who spoke minimal English in Florence challenged me to rapidly improve Italian language proficiency while adjusting to a new culture. Similarly, living in Baltimore, Milwaukee, Chicago, and Dallas has stretched my horizons. Having grown up in quiet Connecticut, living in Baltimore during college offered exposure to a more urban environment, but that transition did little to prepare me for the Midwest. In fact, Milwaukee's exceptionally-friendly people and bone-chilling winters sometimes felt as foreign as elements of studying abroad.

After spending three years with [Investment Bank] in Milwaukee and Chicago—a period during which I absorbed many new perspectives and proactively flung myself into new communities—I accepted a private equity role in Dallas with confidence, knowing I'd adapt to the scorching summer heat and abundance of barbeque joints just as I'd adapted to polar vortices living along Lake Michigan. While often stressful and initially lonely, these transnational moves have exposed me to diverse viewpoints, allowed me to interact with people of varied experiences, and helped me become comfortable integrating into new environments.

A Tale of Two Passions: Education and the Environment

Beyond exposure to city life, living in Baltimore helped me understand the need for a stronger U.S. education system and gave me an outlet to drive positive impact. In serving as an Organizer with a [Project Name], a school-affiliated tutoring program supporting elementary school students, I guided progress across pairs of tutors and students while connecting Hopkins with the Baltimore community. Transitioning from one-on-one tutoring to leading tutor-student pairs enabled me to learn how to motivate others. Sharing success stories of helping students advance across multiple reading levels, for example, generated renewed commitment from high-achieving undergraduates with limited time, and connecting tutors with one another empowered them to refresh their knowledge of teaching tools. It was extremely rewarding to develop relationships with students, their families, and tutors, and to witness demonstrable student progress that often led to transformative opportunities in middle school and beyond.

At [Private Equity Firm], I've continued fostering a passion for creating positive change, albeit for a broader set of communities. Having grown up in a family that, ever-conscious of the Earth's finite resources, recycled enthusiastically and regularly held "shortest shower" competitions to conserve water, I believe the business community can and should do good via an environmentally-conscious approach to growth. As a personally-passionate champion of environmental sustainability initiatives, I was thrilled with the opportunity to guide an air pollution control company within [the firm]'s portfolio. Through this experience, I've helped lead the portfolio company's expansion into aftermarket services, a recurring revenue stream that will boost [the firm]'s financial return but, more critically, will enable customers to maintain their aging anti-pollution systems, reducing airborne toxins and converting waste into usable materials.

Looking forward, I hope to funnel my love for blending art and analytics, appreciation for adaptability, and commitment to positive impact toward transforming how we engage with our planet. Post-MBA, I aspire to join an environmentally-focused investing firm that considers financial, social, and environmental metrics. I hope to strengthen the critical skills of efficiently synthesizing complex scenarios, listening intently to and comfortably sharing ideas, and thinking from the perspective of a leader at Harvard. Longer-term, my career mission involves leveraging these skills to lead an investment firm that benefits the planet while achieving attractive financial returns. Specifically, I aim to create environmental solutions through investing and supporting technologies and companies that reduce waste, plastic consumption, ocean pollution, and greenhouse gas emissions. Art and music provided me with early connections to our shared world history—it's critical to pioneer new ways of interacting with our world that will enable the continuation of art, music, and other noble endeavors for millennia to come.

ANALYSIS

Emma's essay showcases above all that she has thus far led a life and career of intention. She clearly lays out the connections between art and finance so the reader can understand the context of Emma's professional and academic backgrounds that from first glance may seem unrelated.

Emma starts her essay with an engaging but unconventional hook. Immediately, the reader understands her passion for art. But we learn that it's the connection to business that makes Emma's passion different. She uses anecdotes to make her passion seem vivid, personal, and not forced. In this regard, Emma can own her story. Intelligently, she uses the theme of Italy throughout the essay to highlight the importance of the study abroad on her growth and how much she took from it, which also gives the essay more cohesion.

It's important to highlight the lessons learned from both negative and positive experiences; this shows maturity, growth, and introspection, all of which a top business school candidate should have. Coming from an underrepresented school to the finance industry posed significant barriers to entry. Emma was able to prosper through working harder and more creatively.

Emma's essay makes it clear her diverse backgrounds have cultivated her sophisticated perspective on the world owing from living in different cities, having a desire to protect the environment, and blending two different fields together. Her essay ends with a thematic conclusion that makes it clear what she plans to do with an MBA: lead by creativity to solve the world's most pressing environmental issues.

—Natalie Martin

in a way to later join an engineering "Grande École." Even though I knew I wanted to have a career in the field of business and economics, I was convinced that having a strong background in mathematics would prove to be a valuable asset. After two years of intensive training in mathematics and physics, I was admitted to Mines ParisTech, one of France's top engineering schools, where I graduated in 2016 with a Master of Science. My training at Mines ParisTech proved to be the perfect place to combine my engineering and statistics background to the study of economic analysis. I was able to orient all my school projects and internships towards the field of economic policy.

I also deepened my skill set through a six-month research assistantship on innovation economics, developing an econometric analysis of the impact of patents on the success of start-ups in Europe. In parallel, I joined a nonprofit organization aiming at strengthening agricultural value chains in Tamassago, a rural village in Burkina Faso, which further reinforced my motivation to start my career in the field of international development. In 2014, I took a gap year to gain professional experience. I spent four months in New Delhi, working for [Digital Services and Software Development Company], where I focused on the links between the software industry and the country's industrial policy.

Afterwards, I did a 10-month internship within the Natural Resources Management practice for Sub-Saharan African countries of the [International Financial Institution]. I had the opportunity to combine research analysis with project implementation in relation to the development of the tourism and fishery industries, two job intensive sectors with significant poverty reduction spillovers, in some of the world's poorest countries, namely Madagascar, Comoros and Mozambique. My experience at the [International Financial Institution] allowed me to engage directly with policy makers of those countries, understand their constraints and their development priorities. It made me realize how developing countries are dependent on the access to funds to succeed in their development strategy.

This motivated me to join the [Financial Service Firm] Sovereign Advisory Group in 2016, as a way to strengthen my knowledge on developing countries' funding and debt management challenges while broadening my experience in public service and policymaking. I have been at [the firm] for three years now. This experience has proved to be incredibly rich and has exposed me to life changing challenges that further reinforced my career choices.

I have been given significant responsibilities and a high level of exposure through direct and on-field work in several countries in Sub-Saharan Africa, the Middle East and Latin America. Over the three years, I have been assigned to debt restructuring advisory missions such as the restructuring of Mozambique's sovereign external debt. I have participated in IMF Program discussions and have also advised governments on the optimization of their balance sheets, with a particular focus on contingent liabilities and State-owned enterprises. In particular, I have assisted the Ecuadorian government in the economic assessment of several public concessions and the preparation of the optimal funding strategy for large infrastructure projects. I have also recently worked with the South African authorities in relation to the financial challenges faced by the public electricity company. I have also advised private enterprises in their expansion strategies in Africa; in particular I have advised Africa's e-commerce leader, in their private fundraising process, and [Telecommunications Company] in various acquisition mandates.

All those experiences have confronted me with the realities of public administration and private companies in developing countries, and strengthened my motivation to devote my career to helping countries pave the road to a more inclusive and sustainable development. In that regard, I believe that the MBA comes in the continuity of my educational and professional background, and will provide me with invaluable tools to further engage myself and make informed decisions going forward.

ANALYSIS

Maria comprehensively highlights her experiences and the impact that she has already made, revealing exactly how an MBA degree will help her achieve even greater impact. Her hook showcases her deep passion and extensive experience in international development. She further elaborates on this by describing her belief that effective public policies must be intersectional, collaborative, and interdisciplinary. As such, this supports the idea that not only does the world benefit from diverse perspectives in decision-making, but institutions such as Harvard Business School will benefit from Maria's unique perspective and background also.

In the body of her essay, Maria takes the reader through her interdisciplinary approach to education by combining technology and math with economics. Then, she describes each step of her career, specifying what she was able to gain from it, what she was able to contribute to regional and global development, and how each step motivated her towards the next step in her career. Finally, she finishes with how all of these experiences have motivated her to take this next step towards an MBA. Therefore, she successfully highlights the breadth of experience that she has while also demonstrating a deliberate, logical approach towards the development of her career, showing the reader that an MBA is, in fact, the best next step.

The essay clearly highlights Maria's continued dedication to international development and provides a clear motivation for why an MBA would be valuable. Additionally, it stresses Maria's constant drive for improvement, for both herself and the countries with which she is working. In short, Maria's background demonstrates to the Admissions Committee that Maria will be a driven and uniquely valuable addition to Harvard Business School's community and that she has a clear plan of how she will use their MBA degree to drive further global impact.

—Amy Zhou

JOHN R.

Home State/Country: Florida, USA
Undergraduate School: Harvard College
GPA Range: 3.3–3.7
GMAT: 750 T (Taken over five years ago, GMAT breakdown no longer accessible)
Work Experience: Private Equity
Word Count: 828

ESSAY

My name is John, and I was born and raised in South Florida. Whenever I have a chance to go home, I always set aside time to visit a small bank that I interned at during my sophomore summer. The reason I'm telling you this is because at that time, I suffered the biggest professional setback I've ever had, but oddly enough, it transformed into one of the most positive experiences of my young career, becoming one of the main motivating factors behind my passion for entrepreneurship.

At the start of that summer, I received a phone call from the mutual fund that I was going to be interning at. The man on the phone shared grave news with me: "John, unfortunately your employment was planned outside of the regular application season and was never cleared with HR. We're afraid it seems you will have to look elsewhere for work."

It was early June, and I was now jobless for the summer.

I started cold-calling several nearby financial services firms per day looking for an internship, even offering to work unpaid. Nearly 40 desperate voice messages later, I received one phone call back, which turned into an interview the following day. Fortunately, I got the job.

My first day was intense—after a two-hour crash course through basic accounting and finance, I jumped into loan underwriting right away. My supervisor, the Lending Director, was regularly working 20 to 30 hours extra per week because he wanted our clients to expect only the best. Everything was due yesterday, and there was always more work to be done. He always said that the best employees could finish work ahead of time without compromising on quality. While it took me four weeks to slog through my first loan, I was able to finish my last one in three days under his tutelage.

While the work experience was invaluable, there was something else I gained even more from. Whenever I received a new loan, I would ask my supervisor for some background information on the client. The stories added a dimension of depth and significance to each request. For example, there was a real estate agent who was the son of a single mother in Queens and moved down to the area a couple of decades ago to start his business from scratch. There was an investor from my neighborhood who also attended Harvard, and he was returning to the area to open up a restaurant. There was a group of relatively young investors who, while working 9 to 5 jobs, had developed and sold an apartment complex at nearly a 50% return over three years.

I could not have foreseen the extent to which our clients and their stories would move me. All those hours spent in my supervisor's office learning about the challenges and difficulties that they faced in order to achieve what they wanted inspired me to reach greater heights. As the summer progressed, I started to root for these guys—my confidence in them grew, along with my confidence in myself.

As I learned more about them, I began to figure out why these determined men and women were cut from a different cloth. They believed in themselves, almost to a fault. They acted as if failure wasn't even a possibility, and despite being constantly bombarded with reasons to quit, they pressed onward. They had the willpower to remain vigorously committed to building something of their own, and that quality attracted the support of the people around them.

That summer was integral to shaping my work philosophy, and it wasn't because I learned how to discount cash flows. While I certainly learned a lot as far as technical skills go, the most important thing I gained was a clearer understanding of what it meant to have an entrepreneurial attitude. Entrepreneurship is about taking initiative, and by realizing this, I obtained a heightened and more deeply rooted level of confidence in myself. I became committed to being like those guys—someone who would stop at nothing to realize a dream.

I left that internship with a renewed sense of purpose. My junior year, I became more wholly involved in my fraternity, taking on a variety of leadership positions and responsibilities ranging from new member education to community service. That summer, I interned at [Investment Bank] and formed such strong bonds with the other interns that they transformed from being my coworkers to being my family. My senior year, I began working on a start-up with my roommate in order to turn an idea I had into a reality.

I committed to [Investment Bank] full-time, as I truly fell in love with my job. But I'll never forget the summer that so greatly changed my outlook on life. Every chance I get to go home to South

Florida, I'll never forget to drop in and say "hi" to the only bank that picked up my phone call so long ago.

ANALYSIS

John tells the reader a compelling narrative about his first internship at a small bank in Florida and how the work experience gained helped him develop a strong work ethic, demonstrating his potential for growth and his passion for entrepreneurship.

The essay begins by introducing the bank he always visited in Florida, drawing in the reader. He then begins to tell the story about how he was not able to get the summer internship he wished for and demonstrates his tenacity by talking about the dozens of calls he made to various employers trying to find an internship, also showing a deep interest in truly learning by offering to work unpaid.

John lists some of the skills he developed and a few anecdotes about what he learned during the internship to show its importance to him. During the essay, a clear sense of growth can be felt as he acquired the know-how of the craft. Later, he also talks about the diverse activities the internship enabled him to engage in after that summer, such as doing community service and beginning the development of a start-up with a colleague.

The essay tells a unique story that illustrates John's dedication towards his work in detail. Choosing to talk about a first work experience and demonstrating the impact it had on him so well certainly gave him an edge over other applicants.

—Felipe Tancredo

Gustavo B.

Home State/Country: Brazil
Undergraduate School: State University of Campinas
GPA Range: 3.3–3.7
GMAT: 720 T (39V; 49Q)
Work Experience: Consulting
Word Count: 1,170

ESSAY

Sitting in the go-kart number 43, while the sun beat down on the track, I was feeling depleted. Having completed 23 hours of the 24-hour go-karting relay of Interlagos, the most important amateur event in Brazil, my only mission at the time was to keep our pace for the last hour and secure a position among the top ten teams, our objective all along. At that moment, as I visualized the race ahead, I realized that the basic rule of racing was also my guiding philosophy in my professional life: never get left behind.

I come from a poor region of São Paulo, from a working-class family. My father ran an automotive paint store, so I grew up surrounded by cars, eventually working at my father's store as a teenager. Later, I chose to study mechanical engineering at Unicamp, one of Brazil's best universities, where I worked on Unicamp's racing team designing prototypes for national competitions. After six months on the team, I was selected to become the head of chassis design, leading a group of four other engineers to optimize performance. As a result, we moved from 46th to 6th in the national competition in Brazil, which helped me secure a scholarship to study in the UK, the home of the best motorsport teams. In the UK, I continued designing and building race cars with the University of Bath's racing team. The desire to go beyond and meet the highest bars in motorsport fueled my ambition, and I applied for positions on Formula 1 teams, competing against 5,000 applicants for just a few spots. Undeterred, I spent hours learning every detail about race-car airflow and aerodynamic effects and eventually was selected as an aerodynamics engineer at Scuderia Toro Rosso. From this experience, I realized I had the power to transform myself into something more and, through my own efforts and skill, I would never get left behind.

Upon returning to Brazil, I realized Brazil's motorsport industry was too underdeveloped to support a career, so I joined [Consulting Firm] to learn more about consulting and business. Harnessing the lessons I learned about success from motorsports, I wouldn't be left behind in the business world, either. During a manufacturing transformation project for the largest white-goods manufacturing company in Brazil, for example, I led a team of seven employees to create and execute a pipeline of improvement initiatives. When I took over the workstream, it was $10 million behind the $20 million target, so I took personal responsibility for the top five initiatives and worked hands-on with the client team. After two months, we were $20 million ahead of target, with more than 50 initiatives completed. For my efforts, I received a certificate of excellence from the client's manufacturing director, an award only given to the best employees in their company.

Most recently, I started a [Consulting Firm] secondment at an e-commerce start-up, which has provided me with the opportunity to learn about technology applications in business, a skill that will be crucial for the future. As a tech-ops project leader for CPGs at [the start-up], I have streamlined work across applications, algorithms, and operations. In one of my projects, my team and I addressed an order distribution problem by crafting an order distribution logic that evenly allocated demand based on advanced analytics. As a result, we could automatically shift orders in all of [the start-up]'s seven countries of operation, cutting support interventions by 40% and reducing delivery delays by 30%. This secondment has opened my eyes to how technology can be instilled in business processes, improving efficiency and delivering both great service and world-class user experience.

After my experiences in the automotive, consulting, and start-up worlds, I have come to learn about the limitless potential of technology in business and what is holding back Latin America, a realization that now inspires me to gain the knowledge and network I need to transform the region. While other regions advance, Latin America is not developing new technologies to move the automotive industry from a traditional oil-based industry to a sustainable and efficient model. The Brazilian car market is expected to be 15–30% electrified by 2030; however, Latin American start-ups remain absent from over 95% of the capital pool of this industry. We face a large disruption in several elements of the current model, from too many oil-burning vehicles to an overwhelmed infrastructure. By turning towards electric and autonomous vehicles, we will create cleaner, more efficient mobility and, most importantly, save the 50,000 lives in Brazil that are lost each year to car accidents.

For this reason, after my MBA I plan to become a core member of [Consulting Firm]'s Center for Future Mobility and support business leaders to expand the revolution in Latin America. Later, I intend to become a corporate leader in this area, engaging with automakers and creating an entrepreneurial community that establishes Latin America as an innovative region. In the long term, I will expand the scope of this technology so it becomes available for everyone. Only committed and creative organizations can develop a new automotive ecosystem, and I hope to leverage my education, network, and new skills from Harvard's MBA program to lead this revolution. Ever since 2017, when I applied for the 2+2 program, I have been convinced that HBS' unique community and teaching methods will help refine my plans and transform them into concrete business models. During a conversation with a former colleague, [Colleague Name] (HBS 2020), I was enthralled by his stories of how the case study method ensures learning on classical business subjects, such as finance and marketing, whilst promoting a deeper, less obvious development in communication and leadership from interactions with classmates and professors. I look forward to contributing to this community and, in doing so, developing my ability to inspire others and broadening my ideas on how to achieve sustainable transportation. Since the mobility revolution involves ambitious changes, courses such as "The Entrepreneurial Manager" and "Entrepreneurial Failure" will have great importance to develop organizations that empower employees to innovate and that harness learning even in the face of failure. I also plan to join the Transportation, Infrastructure, and Logistics Club, which will help me understand mobility trends and collaborate with other colleagues engaged in the revolution. By combining these skills with passion, I am confident we can overcome any obstacles. I recall that, during that Interlagos relay, it felt great to finally cross the finish line and secure eighth place for my team, even though it required 24 sleepless hours of racing and strategy. The pain in my shoulders and forearms suddenly disappeared, and only pride for our teamwork and effort remained. The learnings from the sport now propel me towards my next finish line and I look forward to the race. Just as in the relay, I want to work alongside others and build the future of transportation. By utilizing my HBS MBA, I am confident I will be a protagonist in the revolution and become a leader that leaves no one behind.

ANALYSIS

In this personal narrative, Gustavo describes his connection to the automotive industry and how it has inspired him to implement more sustainable and efficient technology in his home region of Latin America. Gustavo begins by describing his experience at the end of a long go-kart race and how it led him to realize his guiding philosophy, "never get left behind." Despite his upbringing in a poor region of São Paulo, Gustavo indicates that through his own efforts and skill he would never be left behind, establishing a thesis to govern the remainder of the essay.

In his introduction, Gustavo notes his accomplishments of attending one of Brazil's best universities, as well as landing a competitive position working for a Formula 1 team. He describes his shift to consulting and how he applied lessons learned from auto sports to achieve success and "not be left behind" in the business world. He notes his accomplishments as a consultant, raising $30 million in revenue and earning a certificate of excellence from one company and cutting support interventions and delivery delays for another.

Towards the end of his essay, Gustavo reflects on his experiences in the automotive and business worlds and concludes that there is limitless potential for technology in business. Gustavo resolves to transform Latin America with the long-term goal of "engaging with automakers and creating an entrepreneurial community that establishes Latin America as an innovative region."

Gustavo's theme of "never get left behind" remains unwavering throughout the essay, demonstrating Gustavo's dedication to his goal of elevating Latin America. Gustavo closes by sharing his longtime interest in Harvard Business School, naming classes and clubs, showing admissions officers that he possesses both the necessary dedication and interest to pursue an MBA at HBS.

—Eric Elliott

CARLYN S.

Home State/Country: Connecticut, USA
Undergraduate School: Northwestern University
GPA Range: 3.3–3.7
GMAT: 730 T (41V; 49Q)
Work Experience: Retail
Word Count: 1,097

ESSAY

Six P.M. on a freezing February Saturday in Evanston: after twelve hours of shooting across three locations for our upcoming issue of *STITCH*, Northwestern University's student-run fashion magazine, our 15-person team was fading fast. The models shivered in the frosty air, our photographer wrung her hands in despair over the disappearing light, and the make-up team was starving. We had one final shot to complete on our shoestring budget. As *STITCH*'s Creative and Photo Shoot Director, I needed to rally our discouraged group. I draped warm leather jackets on the models, posed them under a photographer-approved street light, and found a 50% off coupon to order pizza for the team. Two months later, *Teen Vogue* featured that shot when it named *STITCH* one of the country's top 10 college fashion magazines. This experience highlighted the importance of values which I endeavor to consistently practice: advocating for a balance of creativity and business-oriented pragmatism in fashion, taking deep-dive initiatives to create solutions, supporting the growth of others, and establishing common ground to drive impact.

While interning at [Luxury Fashion Brand] in New York, I realized that both creativity and business are pivotal for success in fashion. After a confusing day left me questioning my dream of working in fashion, I walked to the Metropolitan Museum's *Alexander McQueen: Savage Beauty* exhibit. As I waited in the two-hour line, I internally debated the topic. I was the company's sole finance intern and my Parsons-trained peers seemed disinterested in the economics of fashion. If future designers didn't care about the financials, did an impactful place exist for me? When I entered the exhibit, though, it suddenly made sense. Among the horsehair jackets and antler headdresses, I realized these uniquely beautiful creations couldn't exist on their own. While Alexander McQueen created runway art that enchanted audiences, the business team behind the brand converted that awe into a commercial powerhouse. From that exhibit, I developed a mission to help fashion brands achieve success by balancing art and business.

Through its gold-standard executive development program, [Luxury Department Store Group] has given me amazing opportunities to blend art and analytics. These experiences have taught me the value of proactively tackling problems with an open solution mindset. Having happily rotated through Buying and Marketing, I felt particularly excited to advance into our more quantitative Planning team and lead the financial growth of a $75M Ladies' Shoes office. One of our keystone brands, [Fashion Brand], was down $700K to last year. Combing through sales data, I discovered that the brand's historically successful fashion-forward styles no longer resonated with customers. Rather, basic styles constituted our most successful silhouettes and consistently sold out. Leveraging the data as evidence, I pitched a two-part proposal to our VP of Planning and Divisional Director: (1) increase the brand's budget despite its low productivity and allocate 50% of this increased budget to basic styles—a 1.5 multiplier to the existing basics allocation; (2) utilize the Beauty division's automated replenishment system to optimize revenue and ensure constant stock of top-selling styles. With our senior leaders on board, we then persuaded cross-functional teams including IT and Allocation to help transform strategy into reality. From this initiative our keystone brand generated an additional $1.3M in sales, and now the replenishment system is employed across our entire division. Without creative problem solving and collaboration across company divisions, this current growth would not have been possible.

Benefiting from amazing mentors in my academic and professional journey, it's important to me to support the growth of others. I lead training classes for new Assistant Buyers and have directly mentored 10 colleagues. While I love discussing the intricacies of product, color, and trend, I also strive to share the analytical fundamentals of buying, planning, and retail math to excite junior teammates about the power of data. So far, eight mentees have earned accelerated promotions. When [Luxury Department Store Group] upgraded its outdated system platforms, confused chaos erupted. With no available manuals, I taught myself to navigate the new systems and experimented until I found solutions. The company named me a system "Super-User," allowing me to lead meetings training our 30-person Merchant team on best practices. Our team became experts on the new systems, which resulted in an incremental $30M in revenue for the company.

At [Luxury Fashion Brand] and [Luxury Department Store Group], I have witnessed how passions often run high in creatively geared industries. I've learned the importance of identifying common ground and building consensus to enable success and have applied these skills to other areas. I love playing sand volleyball—and you can bet emotions can run as hot as the sand we play on! When

I became team captain, we were a patchwork of different levels of expertise, yielding embarrassing losses and frustration among more competitive players. To grow mutual understanding and camaraderie, I partnered tenured players with novices and implemented a democratic playing-time system. While we're not league champions yet, we made it to the second round of playoffs.

While planning the SPCA of Texas' Strut Your Mutt fundraiser, two teammates on our PR committee vehemently disagreed on whether to focus promotional efforts on social media or traditional outlets. During a particularly heated meeting, it became apparent that without intervention our team would splinter. I asked the opponents to share pros and cons of their perspectives and actively listen to the alternative approach. Creating space for and identifying commonalities in differing opinions got us to a solution everyone felt invested in: we would use influencers to promote the race on social media and news shows. With the broad exposure, the race successfully raised $275K for animal rescue efforts.

Going forward, I hope to continue melding creativity and business, leading impact by finding common ground, and taking initiative to find creative solutions to successfully scale new luxury designers. The fashion industry is a $1.2 trillion global business and growing every year. With fast fashion and an over-saturation of top designers in the marketplace, customers are looking for unique clothing to differentiate their wardrobes. However, many young brands that could fill this market void struggle to get off the ground due to a problematic funding structure: companies have to pay for everything upfront but aren't reimbursed until the product sells. I hope to launch a luxury brand accelerator, like those traditionally found in the tech sphere. In exchange for equity, my accelerator would provide new designers an ecosystem in which to strategically assess, grow, and fund their businesses, encouraging the most innovative to expand. I hope to transform the fashion landscape and help designers transport brilliant new concepts from paper sketches to customers' closets.

ANALYSIS

Carlyn's personal narrative, full of illustrations and striking anecdotes, offers a detailed account of how she united her love for fashion with her business-oriented ambitions by pursuing a career in fashion business. Carlyn first shares a moment from her time at Northwestern University that is later revealed to be deeply emblematic of her career. She recalls one February night spent working alongside models, photographers, and makeup artists, who after a long day of shooting were exhausted and drained. Carlyn immediately sought to alleviate the group's distress—offering jackets and food to reinvigorate everyone. Carlyn recalls how, by instinct, she embodied the virtues of compassion and confidence, demonstrating both the camaraderie of a teammate and pragmatism of a leader.

Carlyn then delves into her work experience with several top-tier fashion firms and the lessons she took away from each. Carlyn fused her interest in fashion with her budding understanding of analytics. She discovered the intricate systems of marketing that empower top-tier firms to evolve into global fashion empires. Further, Carlyn demonstrates that she can rise to the challenge through her experiences at the luxury department store group, learning how to navigate the new program and offering advice to her peers. Such virtues of open-mindedness and compassion, Carlyn explains, not only are integral to running successful businesses but also have shaped her approach to other passions.

Carlyn's personal narrative is nothing short of remarkable. Her displays of highly coveted leadership skills explain her career success and demonstrate that she's capable of even greater achievements. Carlyn views the fashion industry as one with room for growth and innovation, which she hopes to be involved in. Lyrical and inspirational, her personal narrative proves that the virtues of passion, compassion, and creativity go a long way in achieving career success.

—Chelsea Hu

ANONYMOUS

Home State/Country: India
Undergraduate School: Indian Institute of Technology Kanpur
Grading Scale: 7.7/10 (Alternate Grading System)
GMAT: 740 T (40V; 50Q)
Work Experience: Technology Start-up
Word Count: 1,077

ESSAY

Our choices and how we handle them shape the people we become. Throughout these years, I have made my own and the hardest of these have molded me into who I am today. I would like to share my journey through these.

I grew up in a middle-class joint family: three generations (14 people) living under one roof. We all helped each other overcome difficulties. One prominent trait that impressed me deeply was that each adult member thought deeply about how their actions/decisions would impact the larger family. In early 2014, seven months into my first job at [Oil and Gas Services Company], a deep sense of responsibility towards broader communities that my family ingrained helped me make my first professional hard choice. I was assigned to execute a critical well-perforation for a client. Upon reaching the oil rig, I saw that multiple safety guidelines were being violated. The moral duty of protecting the workers and their family who depend on them prompted me to go beyond my role and stop all operations until safety issues were fixed. The decision was a hard one and entailed risking $80,000 per day in fees as well as reputational damage with the client, but I persisted with my inherited way of life. Leveraging the attention of Client-HQ that this stoppage caused, I highlighted the endemic safety neglect and communicated the gravity of the situation. This eventually led the client to convince their rig contractor to invest in new equipment and reinforce safety norms—interventions which reduced accident probability by five times. Fearlessly bringing my values into the workplace, I prioritized the safety of 50 workmen over profits and schedule. The hard choice instilled a certain courage to convince stakeholders and initiate change.

Riding on such courage, I made many pivotal hard choices later. In 2014, on a chance visit to Bangalore to meet friends, I saw the game-changing manners in which tech start-ups were improving experiences and conveniences for businesses and consumers alike. Keen to partake in this technology phenomenon and the impact it would create, I made the hard choice of going against my family's advice, taking a 50% pay-cut and quitting [Oil and Gas Services Company] to join a fledgling tech start-up. The transition was tough, but living it I learned to teach myself new things, seek mentors, and eventually transformed my working style from a "process following engineer" to "an iterative, entrepreneurial leader who figures out the right thing to do." The hard choice cultivated agility and aptitude to navigate uncertainties. The most pivotal of such uncertainties involved [the start-up]'s "chat-based" super-app, [Chat-Based App]. Even after 12 months of launch, [the app] was suffering from unsustainable economics and low user-retention. 100+ user interviews I led personally revealed that users did not want a "chat-assisted" way of accessing services. They wanted a service that would list all the major internet services (cabs, deals, bill payments, etc.) at one place as an upfront choice ("choice-based" user experience [UX]). Socializing this evidence of eventual failure with [the start-up]'s leadership, I drove unanimous consensus to shut down [the app], which involved letting go of 200+ employees and ending an initiative for which we raised $16 million in funding. Putting the hard choice to play, the team and I implemented a three-month severance package and leveraged help from recruiting agencies to place 95% of our laid-off employees within 90 days. Overhauling the product and business operations, we moved to a choice-based UX product offering, which became 20X [the previous product]. In eight months, [the new app] achieved over 100 thousand transactions per day and was later acquired by Amazon for $50 million. Effecting this hard choice taught me to communicate, own, and manage failures. The entire journey of acknowledging our failure publicly, communicating it to the team and investors, and pivoting to a commercially viable business model provided invaluable lessons in finding product-market fit and tactical approaches to "pivot" business models in early-stage start-ups.

Finally, with the desire to work on a larger scale as I moved to [Unicorn Growth-Stage Technology Company], I found myself in a circumstance where my choice wasn't about what to do but how to do it. In 2018, my newly formed five-member central strategy team was tasked with developing an execution plan to transform their $400 million advertising business from "service-oriented" to "product-first" (programmatic advertising). 60% global mobile ad-dollars were spent on product (programmatic) platforms and [the company] had started losing customers to competition. The transformation was critical and my team's blueprint for it had failed to gain buy-in from their vivacious regional leaders. One-on-one conversations with regional leaders helped me realize that they viewed central planning and execution as loss of authority. With an open mind, I highlighted the concerns of regional leaders and pushed both our CEO and my team to decentralize the transformation effort. This was not easy. Decentralized execution could be a logistics and communications nightmare waiting to go wrong. However, I realized that decentralization was instrumental to reserving the aspirations of regional leaders and thus [the company]'s famed entrepreneurial culture. To seamlessly manage multiple individual plans across seven sub-businesses in five regions, I instituted semi-weekly status checks and created a firm governance platform to measure progress. Working collaboratively with the regional team, we identified 100+ regional-level levers across supply, demand, and product to build a regional-level transformation plan. With such collaborative approaches we together overachieved our targets and 60% of our ad-business today is programmatic. Adopting this "you drive, we support" approach we achieved more than a transformation. We preserved our corporate culture.

Advocating for and executing the harder but the right choice taught me how to find "middle-ground" on critical and conflicting corporate issues and nurture relationships beyond my age. My experiences so far have helped me appreciate the choices leaders have to make to grow and improve organizations. Sharing learnings from my choices with [multiple start-ups]' founders and mentoring the start-ups opened my eyes to the struggles burgeoning B2B-tech start-ups face. With minimal mentorship and relatively miniscule venture capital flow, India's 2500+ B2B-tech start-ups struggle with creating effective business models and minimum viable products. Applying my experience, I want to catalyze this B2B-tech revolution and accelerate India's ascent to becoming the B2B-tech hub for emerging market business. HBS will provide tools to make and live this hard choice. Diving deep into 500+ case studies and debating with accomplished peers will evolve me into a full-stack leader—one who can help founders make and navigate their hard choices. [HBS Alum] '21 (Ex-colleague) & [HBS Alum] '17 described their HBS experiences as deeply reflective and transformative, and I am keen to begin mine.

ANALYSIS

The author begins his essay with a statement of personal philosophy: "Our choices and how we handle them shape the people we become." This opening serves to both catch the reader's attention and summarize the thesis of his narrative. This thesis is particularly strong because it succinctly demonstrates a sense of personal responsibility that will prove critical to success as an HBS alum.

The author demonstrates how he has practiced his personal philosophy throughout his career. His choices to prioritize worker safety, lead a successful redesign, and secure severance packages for former employees are excellent examples of his ability to make decisions under pressure. His inclusion of numerical markers of success, like his $50 million acquisition deal and the transition to 60 percent programmatic advertising, shows the precise and indisputable positive effect of his leadership.

In his conclusion, the author restates his thesis that "advocating for and executing the harder but the right choice" throughout his business career has transformed him into a skilled decision-maker. He describes the impetus behind his application in the context of wanting to revolutionize the business-to-business tech start-up industry in India, which sets him apart from other applicants as a leader with impressive goals and a strong track record to back up his ambitions.

Overall, this essay has a strong thesis indicating a philosophy of personal responsibility, a coherent and concrete description of the business experiences that support this philosophy, and a clear and unique goal that could be accomplished through an HBS education.

—Matt Multari

KEVIN R.

Home State/Country: Canada
Undergraduate School: Undisclosed
GPA Range: 3.7–4.0
GMAT: 720 T (39V; 49Q)
Work Experience: Private Equity
Word Count: 759

ESSAY

"Can you imagine Uber without roads, FedEx without airports, and Google without access to the internet?" This was the question posed by one of my undergraduate professors as he started his class in Managing Businesses in Developing Economies that has deeply resonated with me to this date.

Throughout the semester, we explored the challenges faced by businesses in developing economies, particularly with respect to the role public-private joint ventures play in accelerating international development. The course was a transformative learning experience. I studied the challenges facing developing nations and explored how the problem is rooted in a lack of the adequate infrastructure required to lay the foundation for an advanced economy to flourish. Given my background as an immigrant from an impoverished nation, I have witnessed firsthand the impact this has on the people of such regions. Determined to champion this cause, I began working at a firm developing Latin America's first smart city.

Throughout my career, I have worked to advance the development of smart cities. As the head of the foreign investment division, my job was to procure investments from institutional investors. Leading a talented team with diverse perspectives, we were able to overcome the key challenge of persuading investors to invest in a politically and economically risky nation in Latin America. Through our collaborative work, we have procured billions of dollars of leads thus far. However, through my various interactions with both investors and the firm's executives, I realized that there is a stark dichotomy between what I originally believed was the purpose of smart cities and the actual direction they are headed towards.

When I first started, I envisioned smart cities as a vehicle for positive change in the world. Indeed, I have come to witness how my contributions are projected to create hundreds of thousands of jobs and increase living standards in the region. Despite this, my experiences in the industry have also proved to me the dangers that lie before us. As I sat in on meetings with potential investors, I came to realize that they were focused entirely on obtaining short-term gains through data collection efforts and not the long-term potential value that comes with developing an economy. With investors primarily concerned with this inherent big data capacity of the infrastructure underlying smart cities, the direction these cities are headed towards is alarming. Today, we are troubled with privacy concerns, yet we move towards a society where private businesses create cities that track every step of their population. Clearly, without the appropriate approach, smart cities could lead us into an era where privacy becomes a thing of fictitious belief.

Despite my efforts to communicate this to investors and emphasize a more long-term outlook, data collection remained at the forefront of their concerns. I came to realize that the direction the industry was headed was not something I wanted to be a part of—instead I wanted to change it. My belief that smart city development should not come at the expense of privacy ran in direct contrast with what investors believed and, thus, what was driving the industry. Understanding that my role did not provide me with the capacity to solve this problem, I saw this as an opportunity to leave my position and develop the skills required to do so.

This is not to say that the pursuit of smart city development should be abandoned. Rather, I believe smart cities should be developed with the goal of accelerating international development by incentivizing public-private joint ventures. As we depart from the traditional notion of the public sector as the sole party in international development, smart cities allow us to explore how businesses and governments can come together to address such needs. With this comes an opportunity to develop and expand the private sector. Consequently, I look to progress my career by one day being at the forefront of creating these smart cities across developing nations. I envision creating such cities not with the goal of data collection, but rather with a goal of increasing living standards. HBS will provide me with the quintessential platform to champion this cause. By further exploring this pressing issue with world renowned scholars in the field, I will be able to think about the future of developing cities, growing businesses, and implementing this change in developing nations. With guidance from these esteemed scholars and my future classmates, I believe the skills, knowledge, and resources I would attain while at HBS would serve as a bridge to the future leader I am striving to become.

ANALYSIS

In this comprehensive essay, Kevin details the achievements of his career and the difficult, high-level decisions that he made along the way. Kevin begins his essay in medias res and immediately hooks readers by posing essential questions that set the stage for the rest of Kevin's essay. These questions force the reader to consider how important infrastructure is to both economic development and widespread innovation, which simultaneously conveys Kevin's mission to help build ethical and sustainable smart cities.

In the body of his essay, Kevin makes a clear case as to why he is applying to Harvard Business School. While his previous job of recruiting investors to help develop Latin American smart cities had a large impact, this development was more focused on data collection rather than long-term, sustainable economic development. Kevin recognizes this and notes that it was an opportunity to build necessary skills. Through direct experience leading a team and raising billions of dollars, Kevin has demonstrated his ability to succeed in business at the highest level, but it is Kevin's explanation as to why he wants to attend HBS that makes a strong case as to why he should be admitted.

Kevin concludes his essay by restating his reason for applying to Harvard Business School: it can be a "quintessential platform to champion this cause" of changing the development of smart cities for the better. Kevin's essay demonstrates a high level of fluency with advanced business concepts and provides a clear reason as to why he wants to attend HBS. In short, HBS will be "a bridge to the future leader [he is] striving to become."

—Sam Carter

T.T.

Home State/Country: Japan
Undergraduate School: Northwestern University
GPA Range: 3.3–3.7
GMAT: 740 T (41V; 50Q)
Work Experience: Technology
Word Count: 1,118

ESSAY

I'm in an unfamiliar situation. I have never met any of these people.
I am at a churrasco—Brazilian barbeque—at a friend of a friend's
cousin's godmother's house for Mother's Day in the outskirts of São
Paulo, 11,510 miles away from my hometown. Everyone speaks Portuguese, a language I started learning only three months ago. We're
drinking caipirinhas, and the hosts are trying to convince me to
root for Palmeiras over their São Paulo rivals in football.

Thankfully, I've been in unfamiliar environments many times before. I am an expert at what the CEO of my former employer calls
"jumping into the abyss." I have dived into new regions, languages,
tasks, and industries countless times, and when I decide to seize an
opportunity, it's at full force.

For example, when I realized I needed management consulting
skills, I turned down an offer from a secure, high-paying financial
job back home to pursue a high-risk, lower-paying position with a
boutique consulting firm in the recently defaulted [Developing
Country]. Later, instead of going back home to work in consulting, I instead joined [Start-up], a high-risk seed-funded on-demand

delivery start-up based out of [another Developing Country]. My willingness to take this risk paid off in the form of operations skills, technology project management experience, and exposure to top venture capitalists. This now helps me lead meetings I wouldn't even be able to attend as a junior employee back home and pushes me to soon take my ultimate leap: starting my own fintech company.

These leaps aren't easy. It's not fun to restart with no friends or to push my intrinsically-introverted self to be extroverted. When I call my mother, she asks the same questions: "When are you coming back? Why are you there? It's so far!" I understand her questions because on the surface, my choices don't make sense. My home country's conservative culture encourages people to stay home and follow the rules, yet I've done the exact opposite. There is little precedent for what I am doing and few people back home really understand it.

My father, however, does. He too left home, chasing an opportunity in [another Developing Country] 40 years ago. At the time his friends, relatives, and coworkers laughed at him, but the skills that he acquired allowed him to eventually build his own company in [the country]: it was the best decision he has ever made. He taught me the value of seeing the world, taking risks, and sacrificing personal comfort for opportunity. I also learned that the greatest opportunities require bold decisions in the face of uncertainty, decisions I'm now ready to take professionally and personally so I can create the most impact.

As with my father's, my own challenges have been worth it. Through hard work and dedication, my former employer is now the region's fastest growing start-up, growing from a small, seed-funded start-up to [the country]'s first tech unicorn during my tenure. Over two years, as Director of Special Projects, I did a bit of everything: managing all Facebook and Google campaigns in the region, recruiting 20,000+ couriers while lowering the cost of acquisition by 26%, lowering customer support response times by 32%, increasing customer support satisfaction by 40%, and increasing courier productivity by 21%. Each project is a mini abyss in itself, with a new area and team to dive into. By the time I hand in this essay, I'll have moved on to a new problem—each day I'm learning something new, gaining entrepreneurial skills, and expanding my network.

These experiences have provided the confidence to dive into starting my company, inspired by my previous experience as the President of a student-run nonprofit providing essential school supplies to underprivileged children. After witnessing the organization's grant-writing process and necessary fundraising activities, I understood how the nonprofit world is full of passionate organizations fighting over the same sources of government and private funding. This showed me that I could create the most impact by supporting all of these organizations—optimizing the industry and systematically enlarging key sources of funding. I believe that by using cryptocurrencies to track payment transactions, I can develop a reliable platform allowing users to follow their donations through the NGO as if they were following a UPS package. This solution would solve the lack of transparency in NGO donations, a sorely unaddressed issue, limiting corruption and unwarranted spending, and in turn boosting donor confidence and enhancing the number of potential donations. This added value will then allow my company to take a higher percentage commission, allowing it to become a profitable social business.

To accomplish this however, I need an HBS MBA. First, academically, the HBS case method will provide the perfect preparation ahead of maneuvering my company through complex situations with incomplete information. This will be useful not only in the early-stage start-up phase, but throughout my career as the company continues to scale and the types of problems I face constantly shift. Through daily discussions with talented peers with expertise across all industries, I'll be challenged intellectually while also developing relationships with individuals similarly interested in entrepreneurship. Second, I'll gain access to world-class entrepreneurial resources such as the Rock Accelerator, where I'll improve my start-up pitch, i-lab, where I can collaborate with entrepreneurs from different colleges, and Entrepreneurs-in-Residence, where I can learn and receive mentorship advice from successful entrepreneurs. Classes such as "Launching Technology Ventures" with renowned ex-entrepreneur professors like [HBS Professor] will also be crucial, teaching me efficient product development with limited resources—a critical skill set fundamental to my former employer's success. Finally, I will access Harvard's top technical talent, allowing me to find a technical co-founder. Due to the complexity of my payment solution, I need my own John Collison—Harvard College, co-founder of Stripe, who has completely reinvented the electronic payments industry—to lead the technical aspects of product development. Jumping into the abyss has made me into a well-rounded polyglot businessman with a strong network, and the ability to work with everyone from C-level clients to delivery men.

Constantly leaping into the unknown has developed my confidence and prepared me to now do what my father did four decades ago: build a new company. I want to combine my unique background with HBS' resources to build my social fintech business idea, eventually developing several social businesses, across several geographies, to redefine the way in which the private and public sector intersect to solve important social problems. Even though this is further uncharted territory for me, I view it as another leap just like the many others that I have done before.

ANALYSIS

T.T. demonstrates an ability to thrive in situations outside of his comfort zone on both a personal and a professional level. His hook draws the reader in as T.T. navigates uncertain situations and adapts to new environments—skills that he has developed through work in management consulting and start-up endeavors. Towards the end of the introduction, T.T. reveals his entrepreneurial mindset and goal of starting his own fintech company.

In the body of his narrative, T.T. uses a series of anecdotes to demonstrate that he is well equipped with a versatile toolkit of skills necessary for entrepreneurial success. First, through making the leap to work on "a high-risk seed-funded on-demand delivery start-up," T.T. cements his leadership skills. T.T. indicates the inspiration behind his willingness to make "bold decisions in the face of uncertainty": his father. T.T. also displays a propensity for problem-solving by breaking down his solution to improve transparency and thus relationships with NGO donors. This last example allows T.T. to seamlessly reveal his ability and substantial desire to address social problems at the intersection of the private and public sectors.

Lastly, the conclusion of T.T.'s essay is very straightforward and connects his goals to the necessity of attending Harvard Business School. T.T. has problem-solving aptitude to handle the HBS academic case method and a desire to hone that skill to be useful when facing shifting entrepreneurial challenges. He also indicates that he has done his homework on HBS and points to specific resources, such as access to workspaces and expert professors that cultivate entrepreneurial endeavors. T.T. coherently ends his essay by tying it back to his main quality: his ability to leap into unfamiliar situations armed with a plethora of applicable skills.

—Taia Cheng

SHUAI G.

Home State/Country: China
Undergraduate School: Nankai University
GPA Range: 3.7–4.0
GRE: 335 T (165V; 170Q)
Work Experience: Fast-Moving Consumer Goods (FMCG),
Technology
Word Count: 911

ESSAY

"Raise your medal and smile!" Facing over 200 talented IT students each sitting at their desktops in a huge competition space, I, standing on the stage, spent a while locating my parents' camera.

This was the first computer competition I participated in. As a nine-year-old, I obtained the third highest score and became the youngest winner to win the first prize. Since then, the IT competition certificates began to decorate the wall of my room. IT has accompanied my childhood since 1998, when my father bought me a desktop as a birthday gift. In the early stage, countless weekends witnessed me practicing typing, exploring different functions, and learning coding from BASIC to C++.

As I dove deeper, I started leveraging the Internet to reach certain goals, such as raising 183,000 USD for my best friend in college to receive the best medical treatment for non-Hodgkin's lymphoma. It exposed me to the inexhaustible power of the Internet and motivated me to achieve the potential of it. This desire drove me to join [Consumer Goods Corporation], a traditional FMCG company with an ambition to win in digital transformation, as the brand manager of [Oral Hygiene Brand].

At that time, the Chinese market was dominated by local brands, which were gaining market shares quickly with a price advantage in e-commerce. As a result, [the brand], imported from Germany with high cost driven by its global supply chain, suffered a slump in sales performance. To regain the momentum, I led a multifunctional team and agencies to conduct consumer research and competitor benchmark analysis, discovering that although pricing was an important purchasing driver, consumers online were increasingly willing to pay for "personalized products." Sensing the market opportunities behind this trend, I launched a Constellation Personalization campaign, where I led the supply chain team to develop a personalization product package including customized accessories made in China and organized the IT team and agencies to design an online program. With this program, consumers could choose their own constellations, preferred graphic types, and favorite colors among 180 choices, as well as print their names and a one-sentence memo on power brush travel boxes. Within 24 hours after receiving orders, the Chinese [Consumer Goods Corporation] plant would send the unique products directly to consumers.

My innovative campaign successfully turned around the business, with the sales volume of personalized super-premium power brushes decoupling that of previous months, and the market shares increasing by 6.8% immediately after the campaign was launched. Impressed by the result, the management assigned me to lead the integrated marketing campaign with [Entertainment and Media Conglomerate] IPs. By imprinting [the conglomerate]'s characters' memos on brush handles, customizing IP packages and gift accessories, and innovating IP-related campaigns, we not only converted IP fans into brand-new users, but even won over 20 awards, including the "Oscars" reward in global licensing industries, LIMA Licensed Product of the Year—Hard Line.

Never satisfied with the achievement, I reapplied the online successful model for pasting business to offline customers, selling out of stock and turning around the negative growth to double sales in our main customer nationally. As IP cooperation worked so effectively, it soon became a new trend in both [the corporation] and other industries; even other Asian countries followed it as well. After many similar successful trials, I expected to contribute to expanding and magnifying the e-commerce influence from a brand to an industry, from China to global markets.

Therefore, I transferred to [B2C Online Marketplace] in [Chinese Multinational Technology Company], the largest cross-border e-commerce platform in China. Six months after I assumed office, COVID-19 broke out, resulting in the rapid shift of China's e-commerce landscape. To keep up with the abrupt change, our team needed to engage existing customers, while recruiting new brands to launch innovations to satisfy consumers' new needs and operate this emerging category whose business growth boosted by over 70%. It was rather challenging, not only because we had to work remotely during the lockdown, but due to the less mature work processes and less clear R&R of the 20-year-old young [company], compared to those of the 183-year-old [prior corporation]. As the team leader, I had to figure out an effective way to deliver the project as scheduled.

To ensure work efficiency, I spent one week digesting extensive relative reports and discussing with experienced experts, through which I broke down the project into phases and then into tasks with specific milestones and clear owners. Meanwhile, I built a user-friendly dashboard for regular online meetings, which allowed me to follow up the progress timely. After aligning the internal team with the same page, I leveraged my network to connect with the current Ethiopia president, who agreed to endorse Ethiopian coffee for Chinese consumers. Also, I skillfully utilized the celebrity influence on hot topics to promote e-commerce campaigns for free. By turning the pandemic into an opportunity to grow the emerging category, we over-delivered sales targets, improved contribution from 8% to 12%, and achieved 181% YOY sales growth, ranking the top in the whole industry.

Looking back, my childhood experience aroused my enthusiasm for the digital world and developed my technical expertise, which empowered me to lead my teams in [both companies] to scale new heights. In the coming decades, I see myself leading an operational revolution to invigorate the industry, providing affordable, innovative services for consumers, and encouraging women to assume leadership roles as COOs of tech companies.

ANALYSIS

Shuai begins by describing the childhood success in an IT competition that sparked her interest in computer science and the Internet and how the pursuit of this interest equipped her for her career. The strength of this introduction is that it establishes a sense of purpose and continuity in Shuai's career, while providing a glimpse into her personal history.

Shuai then details the history of her leadership at two major companies. She gives an impressive summary of her innovative business decisions, such as their development of a personalized product package for the oral hygiene brand and revolution of her team's workflow for the Chinese multinational technology company. One strength of this essay body is that Shuai provides clear examples of her team leadership and willingness to innovate and change inefficient business practices. Shuai provides concrete evidence for the positive results of this leadership, in the form of numerical growth statistics and qualitative benchmarks of success (e.g., receipt of the "Oscars" licensing award and ability to successfully negotiate a product endorsement from the Ethiopian president).

To conclude, Shuai reconnects her childhood experience to her success and describes her hopes for her future career. The strength of this conclusion is that it reminds the reader of Shuai's sense of purpose and progress in her career, ties the essay together, and points to the future successes Shuai could reasonably achieve that would make her a valuable HBS alumna.

—Matt Multari

IV
INFLUENTIAL FIGURES

Prajya S.

Home State/Country: India
Undergraduate School: Delhi Technological University
GPA Range: 75% (Alternate Grading System)
GMAT: 760 T (42V; 50Q)
Work Experience: Consulting; Public Sector
Word Count: 1,084

ESSAY

"Never give in to biases, Prajya," my grandfather said when I was socially rebuked for celebrating Eid.

He migrated from present-day Pakistan to Delhi during India's brutal partition, risked social disdain, celebrated a shared Hindu–Muslim heritage and enriched our lives. Though we lived in a refugee colony, my grandfather effectively shielded us from prevalent discriminatory ideologies and passivity and shaped my perspective and worldview of an impartial society with boundless opportunities.

As I stepped out into the world, I carried these egalitarian values and whenever the world was not what I imagined it to be, fair and inclusive, I pushed harder.

I still remember being disturbed by the frequent electricity cuts in an off-grid Himalayan village where my parents and I would stay during our trekking sojourns. To the 10-year-old me, it seemed unfair that we enjoyed 24X7 electricity in Delhi and our Sherpa hosts in the Himalayas couldn't. Inspired to advance access to electricity, I pursued electrical engineering and later helmed Engineers

Without Borders at DTU (DCE). Leveraging our nascent engineering skills, 10 peers and I designed solar "bottle" bulbs—$0.75 solar energy solutions for off-grid communities. As 50 low-income households lit up, I found the most profound fulfilment of extending "daylight" for 250+ individuals and grew passionate about renewable energy (RE).

This desire led me to the Energy and Utilities practice at [Professional Services Firm]. While my work provided immense gratification of furthering the RE agenda across Southeast Asia, I was constantly confronted with stereotypical axioms like "Energy fieldwork may not be right for you." My work for the UN Women project revealed just how parasitic and endemic gender insensitivity was. When I went to villages to interview women on seemingly simple things like daily work pattern and energy use, I was told "women don't step out of their homes." Debating such discriminations with gender experts helped me realise that gender-segregation is imposed early during adolescence, especially among underprivileged youth.

Determined to engender behavioural change among such adolescents, my friend [Friend's Name] and I launched WeRise; however, I soon learnt that fostering gender-progressive behaviour among these youngsters was not as easy as shaping the views of intellectuals (at [Professional Services Firm] via HeforShe). Without a supportive infrastructure of people and finances, [my friend] and I had entered an uncharted territory. To understand "gender issue" and the psyche of the demographic, we surveyed 300 plus students and teachers, developed interactive aids and skits to make complex and taboo topics like "domestic gender roles" easily comprehensible. However, no organization was willing to adopt our creative approaches of "newbies." To make inroads we conducted pro bono pilot workshops and onboarded advisors who advocated WeRise. Two months and 10 pitches later we secured our first partnership with [Social Change Foundation] and two years later reached 2,000 plus adolescents. Later, we pivoted to a volunteer-based model, partnered with Teach for India to integrate our program in their curriculum. Today WeRise impacts ~5,000 adolescents in four schools across Delhi.

The process of failing, trying and finally getting accepted tempered my idealism and inculcated pragmatism in problem-solving. It also taught me how to root initiatives and create a change robust enough to persist. In many ways, WeRise expanded my tenacity, my confidence, and continuously provided tactics that I leveraged as an investment facilitator in the Government of India to solve for larger structural inefficiencies in the energy sector.

From bringing together corporates and SMEs to make representation to ease taxation norms on energy systems to restructuring solar-power tendering clauses to promote fair play, at [International Investing Firm] I identified many unmet needs and provided services and equal-platform to the underserved stakeholders in the energy ecosystem in India.

Yet I was palpably disturbed by the over-emphasis on pursuing high dollar-value, high job-creating investments at [International Investing Firm]. While focusing our services largely on Fortune 500 companies and their suppliers, small and mid-sized enterprises and crucial Intellectual Property (IP) generating leads stayed at the bottom of the pile. Personal experiences of helping a start-up in the solar-energy system management space enter the market had shown me that small businesses and entrepreneurs faced the biggest hurdles, and most needed our government-sponsored market entry services. Determined to change existing mindsets, I fearlessly tabled a proposal I received from [Israeli Company] to set up manufacturing of its patented AI-enabled smart meter in India at an initial investment of $10M—less than 10% of the average size of projects [International Investing Firm] facilitates. By showcasing how [the company]'s entry could pave way for innovations to eliminate 20–30% power losses due to theft and illegal use—because of non-existent control systems—from decentralised mini-grids in peri-urban India and improve last-mile energy access, I convinced the management of my tech-transfer thesis and secured a two-member team to facilitate the investment that will bring to market the first "Made in India" smart meter.

With perceptions changed, I established merits of innovation-linked projects and drove the need for holistic impact metrics to evaluate investments and gradually debiased our investment services. Today, 54 out of 620 investment proposals in our pipeline are R&D-linked and I am working to launch "Renewable Energy Start-up Grand Challenge," the first edition of Government of India's launchpad for clean-energy start-ups in India.

These exhilarating experiences that started out as a mere desire to build fair and inclusive ecosystems, albeit small, provided invaluable tools in designing and executing interventions and seeding sustainable initiatives that have lasting outcomes. Most importantly, I grew confident and optimistic about the willingness among communities and the world at large to change and grow.

In the past four years, as an advisor, policy advocate and investment facilitator, I have witnessed that driving investments in early-stage cleantech innovations is not an easy task due to limited availability of patient risk free capital and commercialisation support for lab-based R&D. Like always, I want to push harder—bridge the innovation-market divide and provide tech-to-market support for renewables to become mainstream rather than "alternate" sources of energy. In this journey, I am convinced that HBS will provide the next set of tools to intervene meaningfully.

In Spring 2019, I witnessed the invigorating discussion in [HBS

Professor]'s Business Governance and International Economics class and was emboldened by how students fearlessly called-out hard uncomfortable facts and questioned ethics and inclusivity in countries' economic growth. Conversations with my ex-colleague [HBS Alum] '21 further convinced me that HBS is the right platform to debate my bold ideas, learn from exceptional peers and grow into a discerning leader who can catalyze purposeful clean-energy innovation and shape the world as my grandfather and I imagined it to be.

ANALYSIS

Through thoughtful analysis and candid introspection, Prajya presents to the reader how her equality-centric upbringing has influenced her ardent passion for electrical engineering and how she channels this passion into producing tangible solutions that ultimately aid the underprivileged. Prajya essentially lays out her professional evolution: she acknowledges that her professional capabilities in electrical engineering and desire to improve other people's lives are inextricably linked, adding a layer of subtle emotion to the essay.

In the beginning, Prajya cites her grandfather—a significant inspiration in the development of her unique ability to see through biases and to appreciate the value of people despite their immutable characteristics. She later touches upon her experience in "fostering gender-progressive" adolescents but acknowledges that she does not achieve her desired results at first attempt—she then diversifies her strategy until her goal is successfully met. Through this anecdote, the reader recognizes Prajya's acumen and problem-solving abilities: two traits that make her an optimal candidate for Harvard Business School.

Prajya concludes by referring to her grandfather. The "egalitarian values" he instilled in her have resulted in the formation of an ambitious, driven individual aiming to learn further through her peers. Their story evokes the reader's sympathy and indicates that Prajya would utilize an HBS MBA not only to further progress in the implementation of renewable resources and contribute to the field of electrical engineering but also to help address inequality.

—Sophia Klonis

Anonymous S.

Home State/Country: North Carolina, USA
Undergraduate School: University of North Carolina
at Chapel Hill
GPA Range: 3.7–4.0
GMAT: 740 T (41V; 49Q)
Work Experience: Private Equity
Word Count: 960

ESSAY

With khaki pants settled comfortably above the belly button and a
golf shirt that's one size too large but tucked in tight, my granddad
stands in line waiting to order breakfast. We ordered the same meal
we did last week, and the same meal we will have in the weeks to
come. The quintessential American granddad, he proudly asks for
a "Senior Discount Coffee" as he fumbles through a pocket full of
Werther's candy, receipts, and spare change for his wallet. Trays in
hand, we sit at the same table we have for a decade. The sun shines
in, highlighting the sunspots on his forehead and his thick bifocal
glasses rest comfortably on the slightly sagging skin under his eyes.
Grandpa had been a farmer, once coarse and tan from manual labor, now unexpectedly pale. The memory of my granddad isn't one
moment. Instead, it blends hundreds of Saturday mornings, some
innocuous and some impactful, all of which shaped the values of
attentiveness, integrity, and grace that I want to emulate in my life.

The setting never changed, but even more consistent was my
granddad's unwavering interest in our conversations. He was never

distracted by a newspaper; our breakfast was a time of focus, not necessarily on life's most important events, but on each other—on the bonds that we shared, the experiences we had, and the genuine interest we had in each other's lives. He made you realize that you were important to him through his actions, not his words, by listening so intently that it carried an implicit level of respect and by asking engaged questions to prompt you to continue. At that moment, you knew that you had his undivided attention and during a conversation, however long, you were the most important subject. The value of a great listener was never lost on me, and it has shaped how I interact with friends, colleagues, and in all relationships. In a busy world, I'm able to connect with people from any number of backgrounds and age ranges because I've learned how to look someone directly in the eye and take an interest in their life's story. It has altered the way I interact with clients and portfolio company executives many years my senior; the shared interest we're able to form drives results in complex work environments.

I'll never forget the breakfast when his voice had an edge to it. Soft-spoken by nature, my granddad conveyed emotion not through a booming voice, but a subtle voice that resonated through a room. As a naïve fourth grader, I had been caught in an elaborate lie for a school project and I remember the disappointment in his voice the following week at breakfast. Not condemning or angry, but a tone of genuine concern coming from a desire for what was best for me. As his story of being a Great Depression era child receiving similar scolding from his father unfolded, it struck me how irreplaceable integrity is, even when honesty is hard. His emphasis on integrity impacts the way I view investing and the way I communicate with colleagues and external parties. I've been heavily involved in recruiting throughout my career and I take pride in being transparent with potential candidates—telling them both the good and the bad. While it's common to focus on the positives and tell the candidate what they want to hear, I know that the short-term gain of obfuscating the truth will be a detriment to both the individual and the organization in the long term. I'd rather spend more effort looking for the right candidate, so that on their first day I know they are positioned for success and they know that I'm a trustworthy resource to help with their development. Though I don't face daily moral dilemmas, my granddad's lesson of integrity still permeates the way I approach my career.

Beyond any one breakfast encounter, the continuum of our shared experiences taught me more about how to approach life than any specific lesson. When we first had breakfast, I was seven years old. His car would pull into my driveway and then whisk us away. When we had breakfast thirteen years later, I picked him up. With a rolling walker for stability, he would inch his way toward the same seats and talk as if nothing had changed. He embodied the grace and perspective I hope to emulate in my life. The ability to recognize and respect people's evolving circumstances has impacted my career as well. In a recent add-on acquisition, the father and son owners were contemplating the sale of their company and it was clear that the emotional ties to what they had created were preventing them from realizing the financial security their family needed. I spent hours on the phone with them through the diligence process and allowed them to relive experiences and share their memories of the company with me. I respected the transitory process they were going through, and in return, they trusted that I could be a sounding board for them. Ultimately, they realized that the emotional tie they held wasn't to the company, but to the family structure that was ingrained in the organization; they took solace in the fact the transaction would allow that to continue.

My grandfather passed away in 2014. While he doesn't sit across from me at breakfast, I can still see him standing in line at the counter—his lips barely moving, but a smile in his eyes. More profound an impact than any project or internship, more educational than any lecture or book, the experience that defines me is a simple breakfast with a simply incredible human. A $3.29 chicken biscuit, a discounted coffee, and a priceless impact on my life.

ANALYSIS

Through carefully reflecting on his memories with his grandfather, the author showcases a deeply personal connection to "the values of attentiveness, integrity, and grace." The author hooks the reader in by meticulously setting the scene and describing his "quintessential American granddad," thereby capturing the reader's empathy from the beginning.

The author extends upon the thesis of the essay, his personal connection to the three values, in the body of the essay by using his grandfather as the story anchor. He illustrates, with an insightful perspective, how he has applied his grandfather's seemingly subtle and highly specific characteristics into his work life. Thus, he shows the reader his ability to learn from his environment.

Through drawing parallels between "the continuum of [the grandfather and his] shared experiences" and selling a client's family company, he displays not only compelling objectivity but also a rare level of care. Furthermore, the anecdotes from his work life show the reader both his business practices and career successes.

The author concludes the essay by explicitly stating the importance of eating breakfast with his grandfather. The powerful diction used in comparisons between the breakfasts and the more traditional ways of learning, such as "more educational than any lecture or book," highlights a strength of character to the reader. The simple yet relatable imagery and the brave vulnerability evident throughout the essay work together to create a memorable piece. Moreover, from a more technical point, the essay has a clear structure, with three separate paragraphs for the three values stated in the introduction, which makes it easy for the reader to follow.

—Ece Hasdemir

Adriana G.

Home State/Country: Mexico
Undergraduate School: Columbia University
GPA Range: 3.3–3.7
GRE: 327 T (165V; 162Q)
Work Experience: Investment Banking, Retail
Word Count: 995

ESSAY

Thank you for reading my application to HBS. You should know that this application is not just for me, Adriana [G.], but rather is a candidacy of three: my grandmother, my mother, and myself.

It has taken us nearly one hundred years to apply. My grandmother was an indigenous Purépecha woman who raised eight children in extreme poverty in Mexico. The seventy-three-year-old matriarch raised me, the only child to her single, forty-year-old daughter. We lived in a half-built house in Mexico City, and while Mom worked long hours, my grandmother and I spent all our time together: going to Catholic Mass every day, cooking Mom's dinner, shopping at the mercado. Yet my grandmother was illiterate; we never had the background or resources for her basic education. When I was learning how to read, I insisted she learn with me. My grandmother never quit or complained. She had never-ending patience that compelled her to try harder. After two years practicing together, my grandmother could read at a Pre-K level. Until her last day, my grandmother instilled in me the importance of grit. She showed me that circumstances do not dictate outcomes.

Mom was always a courageous, feminist warrior. Since childhood, her dream was to escape the poverty of Mexico. At eighteen, she illegally crossed the Southern border to work in the U.S. She found work on the assembly line of a drum-making factory in Chicago. Although she earned more than our family ever had, she realized that without an education she was just as susceptible to the extreme poverty and domestic abuse she witnessed in Mexico. She returned home to attempt what no one in my family had achieved before: graduate college. Ten years later, Mom completed her bachelor's in international relations. What's more, beating one in ten thousand odds, she passed Mexico's foreign service exam and became a Consul. Mom taught me that I need to act with courage and take risks to pursue "impossible" dreams.

All that I am today and all I have accomplished is due to these two extraordinary Latinas. Since high school, the grit I inherited from my grandmother has served me well. When I was sixteen, Mom and I relocated to Omaha, Nebraska, from Miami, Florida. I was culture shocked, alone, and made a social outcast overnight. Nonetheless, I engrossed myself in schoolwork and quickly rose to the top of my twenty-five-hundred-student class. I founded my school's first Model United Nations club, spearheaded a Dance for Darfur fundraiser, and represented my school in national and state history and debate competitions. I graduated with the first Bilingual International Baccalaureate diploma in the state.

When my mom and I realized we could not afford college, I refused to give up on the dream of becoming the first U.S. college graduate in our family. On March 28, 2009, I was accepted to Columbia University in the City of New York. More importantly, I was chosen among less than 10% of incoming freshmen to enter the Columbia University Scholars Program, receiving a full ride to Columbia College.

Grit is also the reason I have excelled professionally from Wall Street to Corporate America. Long hours and cutthroat competition never phased me in investment banking. My liberal arts major would not get in the way of my success as I taught myself how to conduct detailed financial analyses and technical models.

At [Home Improvement Company], I fully owned all the technical deliverables of our acquisition of [Textile and Home Decor Online Retailer]. Without the help of an investment bank, I was responsible for managing all diligence, modeling, and analyses of our nearly 150-person internal diligence team. Like my grandmother, I never quit or complain, which is why I was specifically recruited by the business deal sponsor—Senior Vice President of Private Brands—to lead the business development of the burgeoning categories six months after closing.

Similarly, Mom's courage has continually driven me to take risks. Pursuing my dream of working in international affairs, as a freshman at Columbia I sent over two hundred applications to global UN offices. By summer, I was traveling alone to Lima, Peru, for a summer internship at the International Labour Organization. Junior year, I challenged Columbia's administration for only sponsoring female programs studying gender equality. Championing that gender equality education was for all, I thus founded Columbia's first co-ed Alternative Spring Program with a year-long curriculum studying the issue in Latin America and traveling to Ecuador.

Post-college, as a first-year analyst at [Investment Bank]—and one of three Latinas in the ~100 analyst class and the only woman in my Latin America group—it took all the courage I had to stand up to my Managing Directors to [make them] respect our female colleagues. At [Boutique Investment Bank], instead of shying away from my differences as the only underrepresented minority in restructuring, I joined the Fundraising Board of a local nonprofit granting scholarships to immigrant and undocumented students and leveraged my network to help raise over $10,000 in donations. I will always carry my grandmother's grit and Mom's courage. I strive to build upon their leadership examples and one day become the first CEO in our family.

This is why I am applying to HBS. HBS is the ultimate opportunity to challenge and be challenged by top business professors and peers. At HBS, my stories and experiences resonate with the case study method. Most importantly, HBS represents a chance to be fully immersed in a culture of rising leadership talent. While there are many clubs, activities, classes, and events that I would love to participate in at Harvard, the north star is fomenting Latino leadership on campus. At the LASO sponsored Adelante conference, I felt the power of thriving Latino leadership. The ongoing support from alumni and the HBS administration made it clear how important shaping the next generation of Latino leaders was for all of the Harvard community. This is my core Harvard familia, and it'd be an honor to help contribute to its growth.

Muchas gracias.

ANALYSIS

Adriana highlights how the labor and perseverance of her family has led her to apply to Harvard Business School. The application represents not only the culmination of her own achievements and efforts but also the efforts and courage of her mother and grandmother. By telling her story, Adriana demonstrates her appreciation and humility and where her own grit came from.

In her introduction, Adriana tells the story of how her grandmother learned to read alongside Adriana at age seventy-three and how her mother's courage enabled her to achieve the impossible and become a Consul. Adriana describes how these two Latinas have inspired and given her the foundation to achieve all that she has, from getting a full ride to Columbia to excelling post-graduation. By constantly referencing her grandmother's grit and mother's courage, Adriana makes it clear that, armed with these qualities and inspired by her family's ability to achieve the impossible, she will not settle. She is still striving for excellence, and Harvard Business School will help her to achieve this. Thus, this shows that Adriana will be a valuable member of HBS's community, such that she will make full use of all the resources at the school while striving to be the best that she can be.

Adriana conveys the idea that because of her background, she is extremely grateful for the opportunities that she has and understands the hardships that many others in her community experience. Such an understanding has driven her to constantly give back to these communities, and she has founded many organizations to support other women and Latinas.

—Amy Zhou

Ernesto V.

Home State/Country: Peru
Undergraduate School: Universidad del Pacífico
GPA Range: 3.7–4.0
GMAT: 680 T (37V; 50Q)
Work Experience: Private Equity
Word Count: 842

ESSAY

Is it wise to live your life always inspired by the actions of someone else?

There are three things I would like you to know about me that are not contemplated in my resume or in the recommendation letters you have received on my behalf. The first entails the motivation that drives me to doggedly pursue every objective I deem worthwhile. The second sheds light on my desire to constantly raise the bar for my performance. Finally, the third brings about my desire to leave my mark on the community. To understand them all, I need to briefly describe my father's history and example, which have steered me to where I stand today, applying to HBS.

At the age of fifteen and just a few months before finishing high school, my father lost his father. With no inheritance in hand, my father was faced with a harsh reality: a mother who had no employable skills and three younger siblings who required food and education. With no college education in hand, he took one job after another to build a skill set. Over his fifty-five years of work experience as an employee and entrepreneur, he pursued numerous ventures, many of which failed. Despite economic hardship, he consistently picked up the pieces and provided for his family. My father is the embodiment of resilience. He was not defined by his failures. His talisman has always been: "Family is first." This phrase has helped me find my true north and fueled my attempts to become the best version of myself. My family is my motivation for everything.

I, like him, would like to thrive on my own and look after my family whenever they need me. I am aware that had my father had the educational opportunities that I have had, he would have navigated the obstacle course differently. I am in the position to take advantage of the best education the world has to offer. I know that I need a solid educational base, substantial corporate experience, a robust skill set, and an extensive network of contacts to go where my father could not. All of these elements take time and exposure to engender; neither can be fast-tracked sustainably. With my father's lessons in hand, I need to raise the bar for my performance and get better at what I do, and to do that, I need to aim for the best: that is why HBS is my top choice.

"Never say you can't; just work harder." This was another common refrain in my household. During my lifetime I saw my father found five companies; the first four went down. It was impressive to see how he bounced back time and again. On his fifth try, he hit the nail on the head and has been on track ever since. I believe that perseverance is the mother of all virtues. When life knocks you down, come back swinging with an arsenal of "new moves" garnered from your failure. I applied this philosophy as I prepared for my GMAT. It took me three tries to get a competitive score. Thinking I could achieve a better score, I even tried it one more time after the third attempt. I know my score is not ideal, but I also know I have tried my best, and thanks to the economics and finance major I obtained at Universidad del Pacífico, the almost seven years of professional practice in the world of finance, and the experience I gained as an Assistant Professor of the Advanced Corporate Finance course at Universidad de Piura, I am certain that I am ready to face the challenge of competing with the world's best. I am confident that I am prepared to handle HBS's environment and the breadth of its academic program.

If I were to choose one word by which I would like to be remembered, it would be "generosity." Just as my father lent a hand to his own family after his father's untimely death, I strive to sustain others as they work to pursue their dreams. During my undergraduate experience, I taught Economics and Accounting tools to younger and less privileged students. For the past three years, I have worked with [a local NGO] providing non-traditional education to the most impoverished children in Ayacucho (southern Peru). As a Latin American with corporate, social, and entrepreneurial experience, I am certain that led by a spirit of generosity, I can add value to the HBS community.

"Family is always first. Never say, 'I can't'; just work harder. Be grateful and give back." These are the three pillars that define me and how I face life. I believe that this philosophy is well-aligned with the spirit of HBS's vision: to educate leaders to change the world through meaningful contributions. I am confident that I can create an impact on my family, the HBS community, and in my country. In sum, I believe I can gain much from and contribute a great deal to the program at HBS.

Thanks for being my inspiration, Dad.

ANALYSIS

In this personal narrative, Ernesto highlights the experiences in his life that cannot be showcased in his resume, mainly his motivation, ambition, and compassion. To do this, Ernesto brings up his father's life story, which allows the reader to sympathize with his father's struggles. Ernesto follows in his father's footsteps, aiming to be just as resilient and compassionate. As Ernesto puts it, "family is my motivation for everything."

Throughout the passage, Ernesto showcases his resilience with anecdotes relating to his process taking the GMAT and his coursework at the Universidad del Pacífico. Ernesto keeps his father's symbolic resilience alive in his essay by continuing to refer to their family mottos of "family is first" and "never say you can't; just work harder." Ernesto is also able to highlight his work experience in his essay, through his work as an Assistant Professor of Advanced Corporate Finance, showcasing his ability to shine at Harvard Business School.

At the end of his essay, Ernesto defines his three pillars in life and emphasizes how Harvard Business School and the HBS community can help him uphold his pillars. Ernesto concludes with a thanks to his father, the pillar in his life who shaped his career academically and professionally. Ernesto's essay is compassionate and showcases his character in a positive light, giving the admissions office a fresh, new look into his personality.

—Shiyun Tang

CRISTIAN L.

Home State/Country: Nicaragua
Undergraduate School: University of Pennsylvania, The Huntsman Program
GPA Range: 3.3–3.7
GMAT: Total Undisclosed (40V; 49Q)
Work Experience: Private Equity
Word Count: 1,411

ESSAY

Coming from a family of avid risk-takers, I will stop at nothing to achieve my goals and am not afraid to take risks and make sacrifices to accomplish them.

"Allah Yusallmak, abn!" (May God Protect You, son!)—these were the last words that my grandfather heard from his mother when he left Palestine for the New World. Fleeing from religious persecution, he set sail with one goal in mind: to attain the opportunities and freedoms he yearned for. Two months later, he arrived in Honduras. Not speaking the language and with nothing but the clothes on his back, he had two things of value: a relentless determination to achieve his goals and a strong work ethic. Armed with these tools, after years of hard work he established himself as a successful entrepreneur and became an exemplary husband, father and grandfather.

"¡Que dios te proteja, hijo!" (May God Protect You, son!)—these were the last words that my father heard his mother say in 1966, when he fled Nicaragua for Germany in the midst of

Nicaragua's Sandinista Revolution. Coming from a long lineage of Nicaraguan politicians, my father and his family were among the first persecuted by the rising leftist movement. Thanks to his outstanding academic achievements, my father was granted a full scholarship at a university in southwest Germany despite not speaking German. Leaving Nicaragua, he had no idea that he would never again see many in his family, who became casualties of the country's civil war. Arriving in Germany, my father had one goal in mind: to one day return to Nicaragua as a business leader. Twenty years and four countries later, he once again set foot in Nicaragua, this time as the CEO of one of the country's largest industrial conglomerates.

History finds a way of repeating itself. In 2008, I found myself at Nicaragua's airport, bidding farewell to my own parents before boarding my plane to attend the University of Pennsylvania. Although I was leaving under less dire circumstances, my objective was the same: to achieve my goal—to have a long-term impact on the economic and social development of Nicaragua and Latin America. Growing up in Central America's poorest country, every day I witnessed rampant poverty. Businesses lacked the access to financial and strategic resources necessary to grow, which contributed to high unemployment, and the lack of access to quality education for underprivileged children limited socioeconomic mobility. Looking towards the future, I wanted to have an impact and I had to think bigger.

Since that day, it's simple to see what I've achieved, but it's much harder to appreciate the risks and sacrifices I have endured to get there. I attended the Huntsman Program at Penn, but few people are aware that out of four siblings, I was the only one to move abroad for school. Moreover, I boarded that plane to Philadelphia against my parents' will because I hadn't received financial aid. Fortunately, I ultimately convinced the program's director to more than match the scholarships I received from other great schools that my family had been urging me to accept.

People see that I speak four languages, but they don't know how switching my Huntsman target language from Spanish to Chinese meant that I took on the daunting challenge of learning a language from scratch, which significantly upped the difficulty of my undergraduate years. One year later, I spent a year in Beijing, becoming the first one in my family to travel to Asia and learn to speak Mandarin. Later in college, I moved to Rio de Janeiro without knowing a word of Portuguese, becoming the first one in my family to travel to Brazil and to speak Portuguese.

Hearing that I started my career in [Investment Bank]'s Mergers and Acquisitions Group, few people are aware that it took me four years and a lot of networking to get there. After three summers of failing to receive an internship offer [at the investment bank], I used the strong work ethic and relentlessness that characterized my grandfather and father to finally obtain a full-time offer. Once there, while I worked on industry-defining transactions, few know that often I was the sole junior person on my deal teams, which meant months of hard work and undivided commitment.

Nowadays, people see that I work at [Private Equity Firm]'s Latin America fund, but they don't know how hard it was to leave the well-structured environment of my previous employer to be the second junior hire on a team raising its first fund. Knowing from the get-go that joining a team with seven partners and only two associates meant taking on much higher levels of responsibility, I tackled the challenge head-on and have never looked back.

Outside of work, I founded and lead Lolita Foundation, an NGO that fosters education opportunities for underprivileged children in Latin America, but people don't see the countless late nights I devote to recruiting sponsors and planning fundraisers around the country. I also serve as the U.S. ambassador to a Nicaraguan NGO providing academic scholarships and mentorship to underprivileged children, and I spend countless hours before work talking to [my mentees] about the importance of education and their future plans.

While these accomplishments seem unrelated, I have approached each one with a single final goal in mind: to have an impact in Latin America. From the time I took finance and economics at Harvard during high school, I realized that the best way to tackle the deficiency in growth capital in Latin America was to become an investor myself. I fought to attend the Huntsman Program, knowing that a business and international studies undergraduate education was ideal to master capital markets and global commerce. I also knew that learning Chinese and Portuguese would be critical for my future success, given China and Taiwan's increased influence in Latin America and the Brazilian economy's incredible growth trajectory. After three years at [the investment bank], I jumped at the opportunity to become a private equity investor in Latin America, where I finally feel that I am starting to have a real impact.

For example, after leading an investment in [Argentine Womenswear Brand], I have helped the company expand to more than seven countries in Latin America, doubling the number of stores and providing employment to over 300 people. Growing up in Nicaragua, I regularly visited orphanages and mentored children from impoverished communities. Dismayed at how so many children lack access to a quality education, I took matters into my own hands. Through my leadership roles in [the NGO] and Lolita Foundation, I provide academic scholarships and mentorship to over 120 children in Nicaragua, Guatemala and the Dominican Republic, finally having an impact by tackling poverty at its roots.

My father and grandfather always taught me that I needed to pave my own road by tackling every challenge in a thoughtful and resourceful manner, while reaching out to others. Throughout the years, I have learned to carefully assess the tools and resources I need for the next step in my journey and then find a way to obtain them. I am also truly humbled for all of the people who have helped me along the way.

Looking to the next stage of my journey, I am confident that HBS will give me the skills I need to have an exponential economic and social impact in the region I proudly call home. Building on my experience and learnings from working with skilled professionals, I need a structured grounding in business fundamentals to equip me to transform the businesses I invest in. Besides sharpening my communication skills, the HBS case method will teach me how to tackle different business problems by debating real-life cases with talented individuals from diverse backgrounds. In addition, "Competing Through Business Models" and "Leadership and Corporate Accountability" will hone my ability to think through common managerial situations and to best advise portfolio company managers. Finally, by taking "Leading Social Enterprise" and "Public Entrepreneurship" and joining the HBS Social Enterprise Club, I hope to gain the tools to grow Lolita Foundation and [the NGO] exponentially.

I have a relentless determination to fulfill my goal, and I am confident that I possess the work ethic necessary to succeed in HBS' rigorous program. I can assure you that if you give me a vote of confidence, the sky's the limit for all the great things that I strive to do to give Nicaragua and Latin America the future they deserve.

ANALYSIS

In a powerful and comprehensive retelling of his family history, Cristian makes a strong case for why he would be able to take full advantage of Harvard Business School's resources and why he would succeed in such a rigorous environment. Cristian's hook, like much of his essay, is straightforward and admirable: "Coming from a family of avid risk-takers, I will stop at nothing to achieve my goals and am not afraid to take risks and make sacrifices to accomplish them."

Cristian goes on to detail all the sacrifices his father and grandfather made and how, through hard work and entrepreneurship, they achieved their goals. This parallel between Cristian's predecessors and Cristian showcases that his successes and drive to achieve are not accidental; rather, they are deliberate choices made each day. Cristian has seen firsthand both what it takes to succeed in business and the positive effects a successful business can have, and he is determined to continue his family legacy by using his resources to empower others.

Cristian then goes on to detail his personal story, about how he always chose to take the most difficult—and thus most rewarding—path to success. From taking the Huntsman Program in an unfamiliar language to relentlessly pursuing his finance career, Cristian has unwaveringly strived towards his end goal: "to have a long-term impact on the economic and social development of Nicaragua and Latin America."

Influential Figures

By detailing his personal history, Cristian makes a compelling case as to why he is a great fit for Harvard Business School. His track record of success and the motivation to succeed through business are both clearly demonstrated in Cristian's retelling of his own successes and those of his ancestors.

—Sam Carter

ADRIAN A.

Home State/Country: Cuba
Undergraduate School: Florida International University
GPA Range: 3.3–3.7
GMAT: 740 T (42V; 48Q)
Work Experience: Energy
Word Count: 1,184

ESSAY

Throughout the years, the lens through which I see the world has evolved. These changes in understanding were shaped by my life experiences, and in turn framed the reasoning behind the decisions I have made, forming the person I am today. Thinking introspectively, I have come to picture my journey at different times as resembling Maslow's Hierarchy of Needs theory.

Physiological: I grew up in communist Cuba, with unpaved streets and open sewers. Power outages and lack of running water were common. My family always dreamed of leaving the island, and when I was 14 years old my mother and I had the opportunity to come to America, but had to leave my father behind, as the Cuban government wouldn't give him an exit permit. Most of my concerns at this time were of a material nature, as I had to pitch in financially. I worked through high school and college as a busboy at a country club. When the financial crisis hit in 2008 and my hours were reduced, I opened a carwash at the place I worked. I washed cars in the morning and served at the restaurant in the afternoon. By the time my dad arrived in the United States, a year and a half after us, I had saved enough to buy him a car. The fear of living in poverty is one of my main drivers to do well in life. This influenced my decision to stay at home for college, although my scholarship, Bright Futures, was valid throughout Florida. I attended FIU, as I could keep my jobs, go to school free of charge, live at home, and contribute. I took multiple jobs at the school: digital library clerk, physics tutor, physics lab assistant, engineering tutor, and nano-fabrication lab assistant. I graduated debt-free. At that time in my life, that was what success looked like to me. Today, I see this mindset reflected in my focus on maintaining financial freedom, which allows me to pursue long-term goals.

Safety: My dad stayed behind in Cuba with the intention to escape by boat. This was an uncertain time in our lives, as we had to deal with unsavory smugglers trying to secure passage for him, and then with the anxiety of not knowing where he was. When he managed to leave the island, after multiple attempts, his boat ran out of fuel near the Bahamas, as shots fired by Cuban guards hit the fuel tank, draining it. The sea crossing by motorized boat takes less than a day. By the third day, we had no expectation of seeing him again. The boat managed to land in an uninhabited key where they spent some days until another boat rescued them and brought them to Florida. My dad arrived on the fourth day dehydrated and sunburned. At that point in my life, the safety and wellbeing of my family was the most important thing in the world. This has shaped how I value and care for those around me. Nowadays, that means helping to support my grandparents.

Love and belonging: The year-and-a-half separation, amongst other things, created an irreparable rift between my parents. Through my high school and college years, they fought increasingly, which affected me emotionally and academically. A project group once had to leave my house because of their fight. This greatly embarrassed me, and I developed resentment towards them. One day I had to physically confront my father, as their argument had become violent. After this, I decided to put some distance between us, as their problems were significantly affecting me. My parents separated before I left home. I have now reconciled with both of my parents as I have come to forgive their actions. At that point in my life, emotional stability was what I most sought. I found refuge in my girlfriend and sold her on the idea that my flaws were worth overlooking. I married her, and we have been inseparable for the last five years. Having healthy relationships and eliminating toxic ones is a competitive advantage. I strive to be in the right mindset and check my unrelated issues at the door before I make a decision or engage in discussions.

Esteem: Starting my first professional job as an engineer, my focus was to be the best at what I did. I fought hard for the "1" rankings at [Energy Corporation], which set one in the top 5th percentile and came with hefty pay raises and bonuses. I gained recognition from my peers, supervisors, and friends. My family sees me as their success story, and I am called upon as an advisor for my cousins. I found myself deriving a significant part of my self-worth from my work. I felt at the top of my field when [the energy corporation] announced it was laying off 20 percent of the workforce. By the time the oil price collapse came, I had three "1" rankings and two promotions. The uncertainty went away when I was put on a small group that was "safe" and in charge of ensuring business continuity as the layoff list was finalized. This was very unpleasant, as I helped my friends pack their belongings. At that point in my life, overachieving at my job and being recognized in my field was my focus. I still love the social recognition of working on something important, but I am careful not to overvalue external perceptions.

Self-Actualization: The layoff experience at my company left big holes in my concept of what I was working towards. My work family had been shattered. I realized that I found more personal satisfaction in my volunteering work helping immigrants than at my job. In addition, around this time significant political changes started to happen in Cuba. The transfer of power is an uncertain time for dictatorships, and as I write this essay, Cuba is drafting a new constitution from which the "socialist character" of the nation is excluded. I have always been a student of history, and I am now poring through economic history books and articles about the collapse of the Soviet Union, Czech privatization, and the Japanese and South Korean economic miracles. I have always dreamed of being part of thrusting Cuba into the modern age, but that was unrealistic in an iron-fisted Stalinist regime. That is starting to change. I have looked to position myself in a situation where I can have an impact when an opportunity arises. That brought me to look for international assignments within [the energy corporation] and started me on a path of seeking an MBA.

At this point in my life, I look forward to dedicating myself to the causes I am most passionate about, namely, the future of energy and climate change in our world, and bringing Cuba out of abject poverty. Although these desires and values have come to the surface, guiding my actions and decisions, at different times, they are all present and form the pillars of who I am. At HBS, I expect to continue shaping the lens through which I see the world and to expand my ability to influence its outcomes.

ANALYSIS

By recounting his life using the stages of Maslow's Hierarchy of Needs theory, Adrian crafts a strikingly unique essay structure that makes this essay unforgettable. The first paragraph clearly introduces the purpose of the essay: to examine how past experiences shaped Adrian into the person he is. The word "evolved" in the first sentence would increase sentiment for the essay from the beginning through its positive connotations.

Each paragraph in the body of the essay represents a separate stage of Maslow's hierarchy. While interpreting the five stages, such as physiological needs, Adrian employs a vulnerable personal narrative. Considering challenging experiences, such as his father's escape from Cuba and his parents' separation, with immense maturity, Adrian showcases his valuable soft skills and ability for self-reflection. Apart from demonstrating his soft skills, Adrian also successfully weaves in his professional successes. His discussions of these career highlights help outline further reasons why he would succeed at Harvard Business School. Meanwhile, by also acknowledging the more negative parts of his work life, Adrian shows an admirable appreciation for growth. Finally, by mentioning his other interests, like history, Adrian combines this demonstration of his regard for development with a hunger for action.

In his conclusion, Adrian explicitly outlines his goals for the future. Adrian asserts these ambitious goals as "the pillars" of his being, illuminating his deep commitment to creating change. Furthermore, directly addressing how Harvard Business School and his ambitions intersect demonstrates Adrian's appreciation for the fit between him and HBS. Overall, the purposefully personal essay strikes an incredible balance of showcasing credentials, passion, and creativity.

—Ece Hasdemir

ANGELIQUE K.

Home State/Country: Benin; UK
Undergraduate School: University College London
GPA Range: 2:1 (Alternate Grading System)
GMAT/GRE: Undisclosed
Work Experience: Investment Banking
Word Count: 1,083

ESSAY

When people ask me where I'm from, I'm always sure what to say. I am an African. Born in London, to a Beninois father and an Antiguan mother, I have lived in six countries, and visited a further three dozen across three continents. Despite this, my mental and emotional connection to Africa has never wavered. I am at home in Africa, be it Abidjan, Cotonou, Harare, Nairobi, Lagos, or anywhere within its vast reaches. Hence, I'd like you to know about my commitment to helping shape Africa's future. My future is intertwined with the continent's fortunes and my commitment to making it a better place is more than a dream; it's a duty.

Growing up in Côte d'Ivoire in the mid-1990s and early 2000s, I witnessed the unrest that eventually plunged the country into a civil war, from which my family was evacuated. I remember the constant coverage of the conflict in neighboring Liberia, military coups in Nigeria and the war in the DRC playing on the BBC World Service, an ominous background soundtrack to daily life. Around this time, *The Economist* described Africa as the "hopeless continent," Tony Blair described it as a "scar on the conscience of the world" (he had yet to invade Iraq), and even my maternal grandmother referred to it as the home of "savagery and witchcraft that was no place" for her grandchildren.

In the early 1900s, my paternal grandfather was amongst the few in his generation to complete a high school education. He went on to contribute to Benin's independence movement and its early post-independence governance. Having learnt the importance of education for societal advancement, he insisted that each of his 14 children graduate from high school, and made the necessary sacrifices to ensure this. In the 1970s, my father was amongst the first of his generation of Beninois to obtain a doctorate in France. He subsequently returned to Africa, where he contributed to educational policy through government institutions in Gabon, Cameroon, and Côte d'Ivoire.

I intend to live up to their legacy by using my education to achieve meaningful change in my community. My father's example, in particular, showed me that the most effective approaches to solving the continent's problems combine educational and professional experiences gained abroad, with a firsthand understanding of Africa's issues.

This conviction drove my decision to leave [British Multinational Bank] to join [Multinational Investment Bank] in order to focus on finance within emerging markets and, subsequently, to join the [International Financial Institution] in Kenya. My choice wasn't understood by many of my peers, who initially failed to grasp the new opportunities that Africa offers. Having gained significant experience at two of the world's leading private financial firms, the transition to a development finance institution was a natural one for me, and has allowed me to apply my knowledge to making high impact investments across Africa. I also used it to successfully highlight the continent's potential. In fact, my enthusiasm for the continent's future has helped to persuade others to believe in it too. Recently, two of my friends have moved to Kenya and Nigeria.

Africa is urbanizing at a greater rate than any other continent. African cities become home to over 40,000 new people daily. Yet 60% of urban Africans live in structurally unsound homes, lack basic infrastructure, and have no property rights. This is untenable—economically, socially, and morally. Housing equates to shelter, security, and serves as an anchor for families, communities, and society. It is essential for human dignity.

Despite this, the shortage of affordable homes throughout sub-Saharan Africa persists. In Nigeria, it stands at 17 million units and grows to the tune of 1 million units annually. In Kenya, that figure is 2 million units, expanding by 250,000 units annually. This is to say nothing of the shortages plaguing the rest of the continent.

I aspire to contribute to solving Africa's affordable housing problem.

Upon graduating, I intend to raise capital to acquire a small Kenyan bank and focus on lending in the low-income mortgage market, thereby creating innovative financing solutions for these borrowers. By doing this, I hope that those most in need will have greater access to housing and home ownership at a lower cost than is currently possible.

My commitment to increasing access to housing comes not just from my understanding of the pivotal role housing plays in development, but also from personal experience. As a child, I remember my mother's elation at finally being able to afford to buy a house in London with the help of a government financing scheme for teachers. I can vividly recall the sense of security it brought my brothers and me after three years of temporarily staying at the houses of relatives and friends.

My experience at [International Finance Institution] has highlighted to me that few financial institutions in Africa provide products for developers and homebuyers in the low-income market. This is a problem stemming from both supply (developers) and demand (banks) and that ripples across the entire continent. Recently, while leading the appraisal of a potential investment in Kenya, I was told by the bank's CEO that it didn't disburse loans for houses with a price equivalent to less than $500k. While assisting my team in assessing property developments for investments in Côte d'Ivoire I was surprised to learn that very few of these consisted of mixed income housing, and that several had entry prices of $1m. Both came as a surprise to me given that the average cost of a home in these markets is exponentially lower, and these stringent requirements make home-buying far beyond the reach of the average citizen. As a result, an increasing majority of the continent's urban population is forced to live in rented premises owned by a small group of landlords. I intend to build upon my professional and educational experiences to change this.

I am applying to the MBA-MPP program because housing finance is a public-private partnership. One that intersects business, policy, and social development. A successful pan-African affordable mortgage lender needs to be built on a solid foundation across these spheres. As such, I seek to complement my experiences investing in African financial institutions with a thorough understanding of organizational management and entrepreneurship.

By combining my global experiences to date, with the educational and leadership-development experiences of the joint HBS-HKS degree curriculum, I will be well positioned to contribute significantly to a new generation of leadership: one that seeks to serve the collective aspirations of African communities.

ANALYSIS

Angelique's personal narrative consolidates honest introspection and critical commentary into a gripping account of how one's ambitions are informed, in large part, by one's cultural upbringing and social identity. Despite their travels far and wide, the attachment Angelique feels towards their home country of Côte d'Ivoire holds strong. They associate Africa with the comfort and safety of a home and remain committed to Africa's prospects of economic growth and development.

Angelique traces their roots back to their upbringing in Côte d'Ivoire, a country that, at the turn of the century, was plagued by unrest and conflict so volatile that Angelique's family was eventually evacuated. It was then and there that Angelique first confronted the overwhelming narratives, propelled by Western media organizations, surrounding what it meant to be African. Placed under the often dishonest, misguided eyes of media and politicians, Africa was described, often using fiery rhetoric, as a continent that did not display signs of a promising future. Yet, as is often the case, these narratives constitute only oversimplifications in the place of the more complex truth.

Reflecting upon their own path towards academic and career success, Angelique recalls being brought up in a family that valued the gift of education. Equipped with entrepreneurial knowledge, they hope to create and agitate for tangible change and growth in African communities with a focus on resolving Africa's housing crisis. Their unwavering drive and motivation are rooted in their recollection of both the struggles that they encountered firsthand without the security of housing and the relief it brought to them finally being able to call a home their own.

Finally, Angelique shares that they are currently applying to the MBA-MPP program that they hope will further empower their investments not only into the African markets but also into the future of African communities.

—Chelsea Hu

Tuka R.

Home State/Country: Mongolia
Undergraduate School: Brown University
GPA Range: 3.7–4.0
GMAT: 720 T (39V; 50Q)
Work Experience: Investment Banking
Word Count: 1,131

ESSAY

"Checkmate!" shouted the 12-year-old boy.

As the word from my opponent across the table still echoed, I realized the 6-hour battle over the chessboard had ended in his favor. With this loss, my race for the 2003 World Youth Chess Championship medal was over, despite carefully nurturing my standings in the previous 10 matches. In fact, it was not the first time I came short of a medal, and certainly far from the first time I lost a game that was important to me.

Growing up in a chess family meant the house cleaning tasks would go to the loser of a mini chess tournament amongst the brothers, and being the youngest didn't help. As I surpassed my brothers in chess, I realized I had developed a genuine interest in the game. Much of my childhood was then devoted to chess, as I was constantly humbled by the inexhaustible possibilities and tactics one could employ over the board. Although I lost many games and got checkmated countless times, every loss brought me closer to the next victory and every failure to the next success.

A pivotal moment in my life occurred when my chess coach left

Mongolia for personal reasons. As he was the key pillar of support and an integral part of my chess career, losing him resulted in repurposing my future. To no longer pursue a professional chess route was a fearful decision, for I knew nothing else but the game. However, part of me was extremely excited about what other things I could achieve in life.

Although transitioning from an all-consuming, chess-only lifestyle into a much wider academic world took time to adapt, I appreciated how I was finally able to embrace my surroundings. However, the more aware I became, the more discontent I felt with the living standards of Mongolian people. Mongolia, a nation that became a dominant empire under the reign of Genghis Khan, has little to show to the world in the present day. Years of suboptimal governance coupled with chaotic privatization of public assets post-democracy have resulted in severe wealth inequality. With numerous nomadic yurts surrounding the nation's capital lacking electricity and clean water, it was not difficult to see the majority living extremely impoverished. To be of any value to my country, I figured first and foremost, I would develop my core knowledge and attain a well-rounded education. As the education system in the nation was subpar with little state support, I started preparing myself for top universities elsewhere in the world. Brown University, with its diverse international community and liberal arts education, fit the bill perfectly.

It wasn't until my sophomore year internship at a financial advisory firm in Mongolia that I truly understood the economic situation of my home country. I realized the economy is driven predominantly by natural resources, and the exporting of those raw materials to neighboring countries is pretty much the only source of income. At [Investment Bank] in the natural resources group,

I saw how mining companies of global caliber operate. At [Bio-tech Start-up] working to disrupt the oligopolistic agricultural industry, I observed how visionary ideas become real and make a tremendous impact. These learnings prompted me to come back home to explore what could be the next big thing for Mongolia. Shortly after joining [Financial Services Firm], I recognized that perhaps there is an extremely interesting future ahead for our country, thanks to block chain technology that utilizes natural resources as raw input and turns them into electricity, which eventually supports crypto-mining activities. In the future, Mongolia can not only become a nation rich with data centers and crypto-mining facilities, but also turn into a financial hub with crypto exchanges and state-backed tokens—a grand but achievable vision in my mind.

There is a long road ahead to fulfill this ambition, for I have much room to grow personally and professionally. However, every decision I have made in life up to this point, small or big, owes to the fundamental life skills I obtained from chess. For example, my first task at [the investment bank] was to build a complex financial model of a mining conglomerate. Although the model was built technically sound, the underlying broad assumptions I used had too much noise, resulting in high variance output. Recognizing my error, with the advice of senior analysts for best practices, I re-built a dynamic mine-specific model that better reflected the intrinsic value of the company. Owning my mistakes and constantly searching for areas for improvement, which was critical for my growth in chess, has enabled me to stay competitive among high-performing individuals despite coming from a non-finance background. Today, as a Vice President at [Financial Services Firm], part of my responsibility is to sell investment opportunities to sophisticated investors and industry experts. An especially challenging moment arose when specialist investors from China and Singapore visited Mongolia to inspect the due diligence work I put together for a potential crypto-mining project. As the investors were clearly skeptical of the project's viability in Mongolia, the local team received tough questions around the nation's competitiveness and its legal and regulatory environment. Despite the pressure, I stayed calm, openly welcomed their concerns, and provided routes for resolving potential bottlenecks. The situation was a lot like the many difficult positions I had to recover from under extreme time pressure over the chessboard. The game has taught me to own my losses, stay resilient under pressure, and be persistent to achieve any goal. In brief, it has better prepared me for the real world.

For me, chess is more than a sport—it is a way of life. The game played the biggest role in shaping the person I am today, and it will continue to play its part as I move forward in achieving my life's ambition. Mongolia is in need of educated young professionals who can bring ideas and businesses that will transition the nation's economy away from commodity dependence. I believe technological advancement presents an interesting future for our country with an opportunity to transform the nation into a crypto financial hub. Post-MBA I hope to join a leading tech-focused investment fund, with a long-term plan of launching my own investment fund. The leadership and managerial skills I would gain from HBS coupled with the temperament and problem-solving skills gained from chess would certainly bring me a step closer to getting there. I am particularly excited about the unique classroom experience at HBS, where the case study teaching method creates a stimulating environment with highly intellectual individuals of various backgrounds and industry expertise. Finally, with additional opportunities to grow as a leader working on real-world problems through initiatives like FIELD, I have no doubt the HBS experience will best prepare me for the challenges ahead.

ANALYSIS

In this moving personal narrative, Tuka connects their love of chess and Mongolian background to the positive impact they plan to make on their country through their hard work. Tuka starts their narrative with the symbolism of chess. Chess showcased their hard work and ambition and chess brought their family together.

However, once their chess coach left them, Tuka needed to re-evaluate their life goals to be outside of chess. Through this process Tuka became more aware of the struggles that many Mongolians live through and became motivated to help out their community. Tuka is able to highlight their abilities while showcasing their compassion and commitment to helping others.

During this process to help their community, Tuka is able to highlight their extensive work experience with a growth mindset. Tuka highlights their endeavors in creating a financial model for a mining company, emphasizing the learning opportunities and ability to work with others during this process. They also mention their experience in the financial services industry, and their ability to gain investors from China and Singapore for Mongolia. This example ties readers back to Tuka's previous mention of wanting to help fellow Mongolians.

Tuka concludes the essay with a final mention of chess's positive impact on their life and career. They are able to list specific ways learning at Harvard Business School can help continue to develop their passions and personal growth, such as "initiatives like FIELD" and "the case study teaching method." Through their previous experiences and the resources HBS can provide them, Tuka paints a convincing case to HBS Admissions to admit them so that they can "prepare . . . for the challenges ahead."

—Shiyun Tang

JOE M.

Home State/Country: Ghana
Undergraduate School: University of Wisconsin–Madison
GPA Range: 3.3–3.7
GMAT: 710 T (40V; 47Q)
Work Experience: Corporate Finance
Word Count: 871

ESSAY

Me ma mu Ayekoo ("congratulations to all of you"). My name is Joe. I received my name from my great-grandfather, a French industrialist who settled in Ghana and created a soap formula that was sold throughout Ghana's central region. Along with his name, my great grandfather's innovation and passion for business was passed on to his descendants.

Having been raised by two business owners, I have always possessed a love for entrepreneurship. In the early 1990s, my dad was one of the first individuals to bring the personal computer to Ghana. He aspired to grow his company into one of the largest IT companies in our home country of Ghana. During the same period, my mom designed and manufactured clothes in Ghana and sold them to a growing population of Americans enthusiastic about African designs, encouraging African-Americans to embrace their African heritage. I watched as my parents, inspired by a desire to make a difference in Ghana, worked tirelessly and passionately to achieve their dreams.

As a result, I too hope to build my own company one day. I

became an entrepreneur at an early age. Mirroring my parents, and motivated to have pocket money for a new pair of Nikes, at seven years old I started a venture that gave my classmates a taste of the Western world via imported American products that were nutritious and fun to eat. As an international products "salesman," I sold everything from Kellogg's Rice Krispies Treats to Betty Crocker Fruit Gushers. Within a month, I was selling snacks to students in other grades and made over $500 in profits.

My snack business was just one of multiple ventures I ran in my youth. During college, desperate to pay for my living expenses, I capitalized on Wisconsin's successful football season and paired it with Charlie Sheen's "#winning" frenzy selling over $15K worth of "Winning Wisconsin Badger" t-shirts.

Realizing the role my parents played in igniting my innovative spirit, I aspire to be the same source for others. In 2015, I mentored with an organization that encourages underprivileged minority students to pursue their business ideas. I drew on my own entrepreneurial experiences and helped guide my mentee to a semi-finalist finish in the 2015 Citywide Youth Entrepreneurship Challenge. Recently, aspiring to develop young Ghanaian business owners, I co-founded the Accede Leadership Retreat (ALR), a program designed to assist young leaders with enhancing and growing their businesses. This year, we partnered with a technology incubator and offered consulting services to some of the incubator's entrepreneurs. As an organization, we were able to work with the incubated companies on their most pressing challenges ranging from product pricing to team expansion. Going forward, ALR will continue to find creative ways to help support [the incubator]'s entrepreneurs.

As much as I love entrepreneurship, I believe that the risks need to be appreciated. I have been sent home from school for unpaid fees, have had my electricity cut off, and have watched entrepreneurship almost take away everything it gave my family. In my home country of Ghana, small business loans carry extremely high interest rates, so many businesses that borrow are forced into bankruptcy.

My parents' companies were no different. By 2004, my mother's company went bankrupt. Five years later, my dad's company suffered the same fate. In the Christmas of 2009, I watched my dad sneak out of the back door of our house to temporarily avoid the police and debt collectors. Ultimately, my family had to sell everything, including our family home, to cover the loan payments.

Unable to escape the vivid memories of that experience, and choosing a safer path, I joined [Financial Services Division of Energy Conglomerate] after college. I began my career in a leadership development program and aspired to learn more about how debt capital is provided to companies; hoping to find a solution to Ghana's small business lending problem. At [Financial Services Firm] and [Private Debt Credit Manager], I have gained experience structuring cash flow and asset-based credit products for family-run businesses and corporations in a myriad of industries, ranging from automotive to consumer products. These experiences have illustrated the innovative ways that Western companies are accessing capital to grow their businesses. I believe that these loan products can be replicated across Africa. I hope to start an investment firm that uses private debt to provide cash flow and asset-based credit products to SMEs throughout Sub-Saharan Africa.

It is truly an honor to be in front of you today, and to benefit from the collective ambition and diversity in this room and across this institution. I am looking forward to competing in new venture programs like the Spark conference and learning from the unique experiences and perspectives each one of you will bring to our many case discussions. I will contribute to a positive learning culture by leveraging my experiences growing up and doing business in Ghana and the US. I am fueled by a deep desire to impact Africa's future entrepreneurs and to ensure that their stories turn out better than my parents'. I know I am getting a bit ahead of myself, but if there is anybody interested in brainstorming FIELD 3 ideas, I would love to chat after these introductions. Again, Me ma mu Ayekoo.

ANALYSIS

From their greeting in the first line, Joe creates a strong sense of personal identity rooted in their community and upbringing in Ghana. The introduction, which details their family's background in business and an amusing anecdote of entrepreneurship at seven years old, leads into the essay's main idea: Joe's desire to be a source of "innovative spirit" for others. Having effectively established their motivations in pursuing business early on, the essay then leads into a chronological account of accomplishments like serving as a mentor to an underprivileged minority student and co-founding the Accede Leadership Retreat, which serve to highlight specific, concrete impacts of those motivations.

The body of the essay deviates slightly from the positive tone of these early successes to acknowledge the risks of entrepreneurship through their parents' struggles, yet it remains compelling to the reader through powerful appeals to emotion. Joe also demonstrates a strong sense of problem-solving initiative as an MBA candidate: having identified the lending issues faced by small businesses in Ghana, they propose potential solutions to cash flow structure drawn from their professional experiences.

In their conclusion, Joe outlines their aspirations at Harvard Business School and how they believe they can contribute to the culture of the incoming MBA class, referencing specific programs like the Spark conference. They end with a restatement of their dream "to impact Africa's future entrepreneurs." Through simple, direct language and effective storytelling, Joe balances individual ambition with community-oriented sincerity to leave a lasting impression on the reader.

—Cynthia Lu

V
HELPING OTHERS

Kei T.

Home State/Country: Japan
Undergraduate School: Nagoya University
GPA Range: 3.7–4.0
GMAT: 720 T (38V; 49Q)
Work Experience: Consulting
Word Count: 1,152

ESSAY

"Sing as you play the piano," my piano teacher told me when I was eight. Embarrassed and scared others would laugh at me, I remained silent, and almost burst into tears. Born and raised in Nagano, a rural area of Japan where conservative values are still emphasized, kids are taught by society to suppress themselves in order to fit into the community—I was conditioned not to stand out.

My liberal-minded, Tokyo native mother hoped that I would not be kept in my shell. One day, a local newspaper article announcing the establishment of a drama club caught her attention. She thought that drama might help me break free. To prepare for the first performance, I memorized and followed the exact script. At the rehearsal, however, the club director suddenly paused and exclaimed, "Forget the script! How do YOU want to play this role, Kei? How you think and feel is important!" Confused, I soon realized that he expected me to follow my heart. Discovering fun in expressing my authentic self, I gradually became open and confident. Moreover, I cultivated the aspiration to motivate others around me to feel free, break their shell, and spread their wings.

In middle school and high school, I tried to lead as a role model. My actions, however, while sincere, seemed inappropriate. When I sang the loudest at an annual school chorus to give classmates courage, the other students seemed turned off by my behavior and were just pretending to sing on stage. When I delivered a speech expressing a yearning for eternal peace at the 60th anniversary of end-of-WWII, my classmates teased me about my tone and gestures and ignored my message in the content. I felt helpless.

Lost with how to motivate others, I found a breakthrough at college during research in Manchester, England. I was thrilled to work in [Professor]'s lab with a diverse group of researchers from many countries. However, I was daunted by the complexity and difference in research practice, which made me silent in lab meetings. The bird who was freed to spread her wings by [my club director] was grounded.

"Let's talk. I'm here to help you," said [my professor] one day. His big warm smile eased my tension. We talked for hours about research, British culture, lab members' habits, and all that. He listened to me patiently and gave me sincere advice to overcome challenges. "I welcomed you to my lab since I liked your ideas and personality. Stay bold. We want to hear from you." I felt I was discovered. I regained the confidence to take flight, finally presenting my research in front of the university faculties. From this experience, I realized that the initiatives I took before lacked the spirit of recognition. By considering others' situations, believing in them, and offering hands not as mercy, but as encouragement, I could move others.

Returning to Nagoya University in Japan, I joined [a help desk], aiming to help international students to come out of their shell. Our initial consultations solved simple troubles for international students and, as our sincere support received publicity, students started to talk to us about sensitive topics such as cultural conflict and racial discrimination in their neighborhood. We eventually scaled the activity by inviting around 200 Japanese students to serve as "buddies" for international students each semester. Several professors thanked us as class attendance of international students improved dramatically after help desk started. This time, I did not feel helpless—I found a way to unleash others' potential.

As a business management consultant, I continue supporting clients and colleagues to realize their full potential. When I noticed that a junior member seemed distressed and stayed silent in team meetings, I explained how the clients appreciated his analysis. I also offered to hold private sessions with him before meetings to discuss how to present his findings. He became vocal in the latter half of the project, and his implications formed the foundation of our final proposal. Seeing his transformation, I rediscovered my mission: to motivate others to be themselves.

Wishing to motivate more people, my passion has extended to younger generations. I want children to receive the support to be themselves just like I received. Such support should not be a privilege or coincidence. Therefore, I am determined to transform the compulsory education in Japan, in which children quash their ability to express their authentic selves with uniform entrance exams and lecture-only classes. I want to encourage them to break out of their shells and speak out in their own voices.

As the first step, in February 2017, I co-founded VOICE, a nonprofit organization which aims to create a society where all children can pursue their full potential. With seven education activists as VOICE members, we host workshops inviting parents, children, teachers, and entrepreneurs, involving over 1,200 attendees so far. Attendees raise issues, discuss with panels, and present valuable best practices worth spreading. Realizing the positioning of VOICE to unite diverse stakeholders, I discussed with leaders of other organizations and this August held a convention to provoke larger scale discussions in front of the Japanese government, an initial sponsor of the event. Since we aimed to involve over 2,000 attendees and guests including industry leaders from overseas, we needed financial support. I led fundraising, approaching over 50 companies, but half declined. "No financial benefit in supporting education," "No promising synergy with our business," I heard too often.

I realized that the path to scale the impact of what VOICE has pursued involves challenges in funding, human resources, and strategic approach. As I interacted with other educational entrepreneurs, I realized that VOICE was not an exception. For those who also struggled to fundraise, I could not find sponsors. For those who had trouble managing their organizations, my advice seemed like pie-in-the-sky theory. For those who sought strategic approaches to scale their business, I could not solve issues without involving team members from the company.

Now, I seek social entrepreneurial, financial, and organizational skills to work as a world-changer capable of scaling out social businesses. With business acumen I will enhance over the next two years, I aspire to empower educational organizations and support aspirational entrepreneurs to overcome the challenges of scaling their business. Now, our company advises the government ministry with jurisdiction over Japanese education and has an extended network with small to large businesses. Leveraging the significant position of our company in the industry, I am determined to realize more educational projects with small but valuable businesses to scale them and bring greater impact to society.

Just as my mentors have inspired me, I want my actions to reverberate and touch the hearts of younger generations. The positive spiral I want to create will echo into the future as younger generations grow up proud of their authentic selves and confident to step forward to impact the future.

ANALYSIS

Using an impactful childhood anecdote, Kei opens the essay by revealing her most personal struggle: finding her voice. Though she encountered mentors who encouraged her to be more confident, Kei's attempts to assert herself were constantly met with opposition in her community. However, Kei demonstrates that she never gave up in her pursuit of confidence, which emphasizes her resilience and dedication to her goals. Hard work and a good work ethic is vital for success in business school, and Kei's narrative helps make a positive impression on admissions officers.

Kei then continues by describing how her contributions during her time at Nagoya University helped transform the school's international student community. Encouraged by her results, she continues to motivate people to speak their mind and become more self-assured, eventually co-founding a nonprofit for schoolchildren.

Here Kei explains that her new lifelong goal is to revolutionize the world of Japanese schooling, such that children feel comfortable being their true selves. Kei acknowledges she has much more to learn before she can achieve such a feat, which neatly summarizes her main motivation for applying to Harvard Business School: to gain expertise in the world of education. By explaining how she seeks to inspire children the way her mentors inspired her, Kei is able to illustrate her desire to give back to her community, making an impassioned case for admission to HBS.

—Alison Tan

LAURA R.

Home State/Country: California, USA
Undergraduate School: California State University, Fullerton
GPA Range: 3.7–4.0
GMAT: 730 T (42V; 47Q)
Work Experience: Investment Management
Word Count: 1,197

ESSAY

I regretted it the moment the words came out of my mouth—"Oh, we're the smart kids," I blurted when the Outdoor Ed camp counselor asked what APAAS (Alternative Program for Academically Advanced Students) meant. I didn't mean to, but I drew a line in the sand between our cluster and the others, unintentionally verbalizing what seemed like the truth to me then. Immediately, tension gripped the class as other honors students jumped to defend the intelligence of our non-accelerated peers. Surrounded by whispering fifth graders and pine trees, I became intimately aware of how much words mattered, sometimes even more than the intention behind them. I never wanted to make anyone feel "less than" ever again.

Reflecting on that moment is still painful for me, knowing my words contributed to putting down others. Since then, I have strived to act more mindfully, and incorporated my core value of uplifting others in everything I do. What I want you to know is that in situations where I have an advantage, I aim to use it to empower others.

In high school, seeing my peers struggling to keep up with our heavy class load while the curriculum came easier to me, I created and shared study guides. I summarized our required reading creatively, including attempts at humor and modern slang to make them easier to digest. After my classmates found the first study guide amusing and helpful, I kept sharing my take to promote collaborative learning. This caught on, with some classmates reaching out with questions and others sharing their notes. While my mom chided me for promoting cheating, I felt sharing my notes helped everyone understand the material better and gave the whole class a fair shot, not just those of us with a natural aptitude for school.

As VP of Finance in college, I chaired the Instructionally Related Activities Committee, which allocates funds to programs led by professors. My goals that year—in line with my desire to create opportunities for others—were to engage my committee members in the budget process and drive a more equitable distribution of funds. Researching past budgets, I noticed that some professors received funding, year after year, while others did not, year after year. Frustrated that new programs were not getting a fair shot, I recorded a mandatory interactive training video aimed at helping professors understand the process and submit a competitive application. At our Friday morning meetings, over coffee and bagels, I led student and faculty committee members in a discussion on ways to ensure a more equitable distribution of funds, which resulted in a consistent rating rubric still used today. In our last meeting, we approved one of the most broadly distributed budgets since the program's inception, and I couldn't have been more proud.

When I joined a student investing team my senior year, I was one of only two women in the 20-person program. I was apprehensive about joining a male-dominated team, expecting it to be challenging, but I wasn't prepared to be openly mocked for asking what I thought was a reasonable question. While I gained invaluable hands-on portfolio management experience, I wanted to help shape the culture to be more open to different perspectives, so I started a women's group. I envisioned it being a welcoming place for students and alums to ask questions and share experiences. At our first brunch event, bombarded with inquiries from students, I found myself sketching diagrams on a napkin to explain a nuanced investment concept. Encouraged by the current students' positive feedback, I tracked down our limited female alum and organized additional events. As the group evolved, I saw the difference even small mentorship efforts can make. While I can't take full credit for this achievement, I am proud to share that there were six women in the most recent graduating class, the most in program history.

During my second year at work, remembering how intimidating it felt to be a new analyst without a safe place to ask questions, I started a mentorship program. I wanted to give our two first-year analysts the opportunity to build skills and confidence in a low-risk setting. Encouraging them to schedule mock presentations with me, I offered my time and constructive feedback. After our first virtual mock, one analyst mentioned he appreciated me reaching out as he had wanted the opportunity to practice but wasn't sure how to initiate it. Impressed by his clear grasp of the material, I suggested he work on not rushing, and have already witnessed him improving, presenting at a more relaxed pace. When two new analysts joined this summer, I expanded this effort, initiating weekly market discussions to create an approachable environment for them to seek guidance. From leading this initiative, I learned that it is possible to implement change at work even without being in a senior leadership role.

At the same time, I've had the opportunity to draw inspiration from accomplished leaders who emphasized supporting others.

When I first joined the workforce, I unfortunately believed that I was less valuable than someone in a higher position and I was lucky if they responded, even dismissively. After joining our ESG (Environmental, Social, Governance) team and prepping for the launch of our new climate-focused strategy, I tepidly reached out to a more senior member of the team in London for his input, still half expecting to be blown off. Instead this near-stranger, eight time zones away, made time for me. He responded quickly with the data I needed and offered a phone call to walk me through his thorough written explanation. His kindness and generosity blew me away. That was nearly a year ago and I am still amazed by his willingness to help, sharing his time and expertise when I need guidance on climate-related inquiries. As a leader, I aspire to make others feel valued in the same way.

This summer, when a new account manager asked me for help collecting information on one of my products, I eagerly answered his first set of questions. As someone who enjoys supporting others, I was happy to respond with the information he needed. He wanted to be prepared as he was presenting on the strategy and followed up with me multiple times for more detail. My supervisor told me I wasn't obligated to spend more time helping him, but instead I scheduled a call, recalling my own experiences of nervously prepping for a big presentation. Meeting face-to-face over a video call, we discussed our investment philosophy/process and addressed areas where he needed more material. After our call, I answered a few final questions over email, and his presentation the following week went off without a hitch. Although it wasn't part of my job description, taking the time to see him succeed was important to me.

While as a child I felt the sting of knowing I put my peers down, I have since realized the impact uplifting and empowering others can have. I want to contribute to my community by being a leader who educates and encourages my team. At Harvard and after, I will endeavor to create spaces where my future classmates and colleagues can learn and grow.

ANALYSIS

Through anecdotal evidence in the introduction, Laura emphasizes the personal value of "uplifting others" in her life and integrating this core value into everything she does. She briefly touches on an experience she underwent in fifth grade that served as a lesson she would carry into college. This is an effective strategy when it comes to garnering sympathy from the reader, as it demonstrates the applicant's well-roundedness and moral intuition.

In college, for instance, Laura mentions her participation in the Instructionally Related Activities Committee, where she incorporates her "desire to help others" with finance and business, showing the reader her competitive value as an applicant to Harvard Business School and linking her altruistic initiative with her aptitude for academics.

Laura elaborates on her involvement in positions of authority in college and how she helped develop her strong sense of leadership and desire to guide and support her peers through the means of knowledge. Laura refers to her success in the mission of achieving a more "equitable distribution of funds" as well as her subsequent initiative of creating a women's group to implicitly corroborate what she mentions regarding her creative drive and willingness to take chances.

Laura concludes her essay by connecting her preparedness to

support others through their academic journey with her future valuable input to Harvard Business School, exposing the reader to the multifaceted nature of her abilities, which are not limited to academics but also encompass wanting to "contribute to [her] community" and to "empower" others.

—Sophia Klonis

Sarah J.

Home State/Country: North Carolina, USA
Undergraduate School: University of North Carolina
at Chapel Hill
GPA Range: 3.7–4.0
GRE: 328 T (163V; 165Q)
Work Experience: Business Development
Word Count: 1,257

ESSAY

At nine years old, as I sat between my parents on a train traveling
through Scotland, I overheard an older woman seated a few rows in
front of us shouting at a young Muslim mother and her child. Per-
plexed and feeling uncomfortable, I tuned into the conversation
to hear her tell them, "Go back to your country." Before long, my
father stood up and walked over to intervene. He invited the family
to sit with us, firmly scolding the woman that she had no right to
talk to anyone that way. I remember the event vividly to this day,
and palpably recall the pride I felt for my father.

Over the years, I naturally inherited this sense of social justice
from my parents. As an adult, my desire to fix societal issues grew
exponentially; it became essential for me to dedicate my time to
initiatives that help improve the lives of others. Since childhood,
I have responded to the justice and kindness that has been modeled for me by giving it back unconditionally to others, focusing on
my belief that political, cultural, ethnic, and gender boundaries are

broken down when people help each other and build sincere relationships.

Through [financial literacy organization experience], I saw how providing financial literacy education can create a cycle of success for those in socioeconomically challenged situations, from students in urban areas to villagers in rural Honduras. The relationships I developed with these people are some of my most valued. Later, my interest in the "operations" of a beehive and its effect on food production led me to ultimately provide downstream benefits to local North Carolina community members, my first venture into social entrepreneurship. Focusing on improving mortality rates for bees, I designed a newly shaped hive to help protect bees during winter, improving hive survival rate and impacting local beekeepers' livelihoods and families. It was exciting to realize the impact I could have as an individual on my community and the people I helped, and I was inspired to further pursue my passion for social justice.

My passion for the environment, a product of the love of nature also gifted to me by my parents, made a career in the renewable energy industry my next logical step. Over time, I have realized that renewable energy can not only have a massive positive impact on small communities, but perhaps more importantly, on individual lives. While my commercial success at [American Energy Company] has been rewarding, the most fulfilling part of my job is knowing that I have directly helped people.

Nearly three years ago, when I started on my first solar and wind project in Calhan, a rural town in Colorado, I was entrusted with forming important relationships in a community where massive change was likely coming. As a young project manager, I was admittedly nervous about this responsibility. The project was ultimately a success, and the solar panels and wind turbines are now producing electricity for the local utility. While I'm certainly proud of the massive investment and remarkable engineering work involved, I saw firsthand how sustainable efforts can benefit individual lives through the deep, personal relationships I made during these years of development.

To build the project, [the company] required agreements from local landowners to allow construction on their properties. These farmers and ranchers were hesitant at first—our work would completely alter their hometown landscape. At the outset, I began building a rapport with community members by sitting in living rooms, offices, and coffee shops. Over many meetings spanning six months, I explained the benefits of renewable energy, and as a by-product, began to form deep connections. I learned about Mr. B's farm, which his grandfather started and would soon be passed to his son, and how I shared a love of horses with another landowner. We built up a mutual level of trust, and soon enough, the stakeholders bought in and were excited about the project.

Once we received the investment approval, the community members were the first people I told. When Mr. B learned he would be getting five turbines on his property, his eyes filled with tears. His daughter was attending college soon and he could now pay for it with his income from the wind turbines. [Another] family called the project their "insurance policy"—when drought or a hailstorm hit, the continued revenue from the wind turbines would provide a reliable source of income. Over dinner one night, Mrs. L told me how she was going to use the money from the land she sold for the solar farm to reinvest money into her yak business. One year later, she has nearly doubled the size of her business.

The community of Calhan, Colorado, was forever changed as

well. My project funded a capstone program at a local community college, where students can learn wind technology, the fastest-growing job industry in the United States. Now, via the tax revenue the project generates, the community is starting to receive funding in areas they desperately need; a local elementary school now provides full health benefits to teachers, something that they did not previously have. The school superintendent calls my team his "solar angels." I laugh off the nickname but can tell how grateful he is for the project and opportunities it brings. Receiving thank you notes from these individuals has been a highlight of my career.

I started at [the energy company] expecting to help build a few projects and make a societal impact. What I did not realize was how deeply connected I would become to each community, and how my work could help improve these communities and the people in them. I am now tackling social justice at every level: from a community in Colorado to clean energy at a global scale. I am proud of the impact I have made thus far, and I'm excited about my future work in renewables.

I want to continue my work by catalyzing these projects with greater access to capital and scaling the impact of renewables even further, which in turn will impact more lives. Post-MBA, my goal is to work in the renewable energy finance department at an investment bank. Through my experience working with lenders during the financing phase of my projects, I have noticed a white space in the industry: institutional capital often lacks insight into the nuances of renewables, particularly when it comes to battery storage projects. After spending much of my time as a developer educating stakeholders on the ins and outs of renewable energy projects, I firmly believe these banks can benefit from someone who comes directly from industry and can be immediately accretive to their operation. Serving as the lead on the second-largest solar plus battery storage project in the world, I am particularly well-positioned to talk about the emerging technology of energy storage.

I've been continuously building upon the value system and quest for social justice my dad instilled in me on the train that day, and I believe Harvard is the place for me to best propel that passion. Having experienced the case method firsthand during the Women's Day visit, I witnessed how a different type of learning takes place during HBS classes. Much like I learned from the many perspectives within each community in which I have worked, the diverse thoughts and experiences within every class at HBS will offer me an opportunity to challenge my thinking. Harvard is the perfect setting for me to grow my ability to have a positive social impact. I'm excited to start this journey.

ANALYSIS

Sarah begins her essay by hooking the reader in with a story from her childhood. She talks about how her father instilled social justice values in her from a young age. This leads to an overview of various projects she got involved in along her life journey.

Always paying special attention to show how her projects have positively impacted the community around her, Sarah shows her social entrepreneurship skills. After describing some of her social work experience, Sarah reaches the main focus of her essay: the development of her next project.

Sarah writes about how her love of nature and passion for impacting small communities propelled her to work in the renewable energy industry by creating a project that dealt with solar and wind energy. Sarah also makes a compelling argument for the impact of her project by telling stories about individuals who were immensely helped by her activities. She also quantifies the impact by saying her project is the second largest in its specific field in the world.

To wrap up the essay, Sarah talks about her plans after the MBA and the reasons she wants to attend Harvard Business School. She explains how the graduate program can propel her career as a renewable energy specialist and how HBS's classes resonated with her. Sarah drives home the idea that she is a very passionate and hardworking social entrepreneur with a drive for helping communities while telling individual stories that show her potential as a future HBS student.

—Felipe Tancredo

Chiyoung K.

Home State/Country: California, USA
Undergraduate School: Harvard College
GPA Range: 3.3–3.7
GMAT: 760 T (41V; 51Q)
Work Experience: Consulting, Venture Capital
Word Count: 1,070

ESSAY

I am the product of one improbable chain of pivotal moments.

Who I am today is a result of generous mentors who took the time to invest in me. While my immigrant parents supported me with their love and belief in my potential, turning this belief into reality required help along the way from mentors who provided guidance and opportunities my parents could not. Whether it was gifting me a violin, funding my extracurricular activities, recommending me for summer work experiences, or responding to a message asking for advice, each touchpoint marked a significant step in my personal and professional development. It is almost overwhelming to imagine how different my life would be if even one of my mentors had decided I was not worth their time.

My life illustrates what I believe is an undeniable truth: that effective mentorship has the power to propel people forward and realize their potential regardless of background. This truth has led me to a guiding purpose that Clay Christensen spoke of: "the only metrics that will truly matter to my life are the individuals whom I have been able to help, one by one, to become better people."

I have been inspired by my mentors and personal experiences to invest in people like me from diverse, less privileged backgrounds. My only hope is to be as effective a mentor to them as my mentors have been in my life. At my current firm, I have been fortunate to witness effective mentorship and practice it myself. The firm's founding tenets include aspiring to be the best supporting actor to our entrepreneurs and exploring orphaned areas of innovation.

When asked about my area of greatest interest, I elected to focus on women-focused and minority-led businesses. This is a massive but woefully overlooked segment of entrepreneurs, in large part due to a lack of understanding and interest from traditional sources of capital. Given this focus, I have worked with diverse and talented leaders on many strategic projects, from elevating the majority female nail salon industry to helping drive analyses for a professional development platform focused on inclusionary teams.

Across these projects, I have tried to find that single area where I could add the most value. My strength became applying a data-driven approach to customer-centric strategies. Specifically, I worked with founders to prioritize understanding "superfans," or customers who bring the most sustained value to a company. Most recently, my work led to an article, "Successful Customer-Centric Businesses Revolve Around Their Superfans," that I co-authored with our managing partner. These experiences helped me realize that being a good mentor is not about trying to help across everything, but instead knowing where I can add value and targeting advice to those specific areas.

My most meaningful leadership role at my firm has been with a portfolio company selling a unique organic tea product. The company is led by a talented female Asian-American founder. Inspired by her family's background working with tea, she created fair trade whole leaf tea products to bring the ceremony and experience of tea to people's everyday lives. In the fall of 2019, I was invited to join a board meeting and collaborate on an initiative to help the CEO gain greater clarity on the company's superfans. While the team had a strong intuition of who their superfans might be, the team had not yet developed a common definition and set of metrics for those high-value customers.

Over several weeks, I collaborated with the CEO to develop those definitions and metrics as well as share my findings with the team and implement a strategy focusing on superfans. Recently, the CEO informed the board that our superfan work was crucial in yielding 100%+ year-over-year growth despite the pandemic. I couldn't help but feel a sense of pride as she spoke. However, this pride was not necessarily the result of her praise but the sense of accomplishment I felt in seeing how far the team had come, all stemming from our initial project. The feeling when mentorship results in the advancement of others is pure joy and motivates me to continue to help others.

My relationship with the portfolio company's CEO has evolved into a biweekly session where I have the privilege of working one-on-one with her. Our conversations center around how to continue leveraging the results of our work to support new customer growth initiatives, ranging from improved ambassador programs to product subscriptions. My new role as a thought partner is one I am still growing into, but it has highlighted how mentorship goes both ways. The portfolio company's founder has helped me cultivate humility, as we certainly have had setbacks along the way, and her genuine enthusiasm and continued encouragement to keep pushing forward has shown how much she appreciates my contributions. This mutual respect would not have been possible without shared chemistry in working together towards a common goal. This has been an important epiphany for me that I cannot just rely on superior analytics or insights to create change, but that I need to pay special attention to how I do it. Effective mentorship and leadership come from cultivating self-awareness within me and others. My lessons in mentorship and self-awareness of my gaps as both mentee and mentor are just beginning at this stage of my career, but I am committed to taking this never-ending, yet never boring, journey.

To that end I have one audacious goal, which is to add my own twist to Georges Doriot's thesis: to unlock hidden value by investing in grade-A people from seemingly grade-B backgrounds. Attending HBS would be yet another critical developmental juncture along that journey. The school's interactive case method will help me sharpen how I express my thoughts impromptu and more importantly learn from a diverse set of fellow students and professors. In researching the work of different professors and speaking to members of the HBS community, outside of the required curriculum I am especially interested in "Reimagining Capitalism" and "Leadership and Happiness," courses taught by [HBS Professor] and [HBS Professor] respectively, whose work I admire and respect. Above all, I want to make meaningful connections with others who share my audacious goal of advancing inclusive investment that unlocks the potential of untapped talent of all backgrounds. Ultimately, this entire range of experiences will help me use mentorship to positively change the world by investing in the overlooked leaders of the future.

ANALYSIS

Chiyoung opens the essay with a broad, impactful summary of his life, which avoids coming off as cliché by leading naturally into examples of early mentorship experiences. In this introduction,

Chiyoung effectively sets up his central thesis that interpersonal relationships are the driving force behind success, whether applied to an individual or a company. He seamlessly integrates the Clay Christensen quote to further emphasize this idea of prioritizing human interaction to produce "metrics" focused on "people."

Moving to the body, Chiyoung's focus on a single business experience with an organic tea company allows him to establish a complete picture of his specific accomplishments, the surrounding context, and why the experience was his "most meaningful leadership role." He couples his sense of individual initiative and ability to execute on projects with an empathetic appreciation of collaboration, and the recurrence of words such as "mutual," "shared," and "together" in characterizing his work continues to highlight this theme.

Chiyoung reflects on a few personal takeaways regarding the reciprocality of mentorship and "how [it] goes both ways." He also goes beyond describing his past performance to explicitly outline a goal for the future: "investing in grade-A people from seemingly grade-B backgrounds." Tying these aspirations directly to Harvard Business School, Chiyoung makes specific references to the "interactive case method," along with particular courses and professors, exhibiting a dedicated, well-researched interest in HBS and explaining why he would be a successful student. Overall, the essay is logically organized, emotionally compelling, and holds a clear sense of intent throughout, leaving the reader with a promising impression of Chiyoung as an MBA candidate capable of creating positive change in the world.

—Cynthia Lu

CLAYTON O.

Home State/Country: Wisconsin, USA
Undergraduate School: Undisclosed
GPA Range: 3.3–3.7
GMAT: 730 T (44V; 47Q)
Work Experience: Investment Banking
Word Count: 1,087

ESSAY

My favorite family picture includes me at six years old sitting on a small motocross bike in the backyard of my childhood home. My mom is standing behind me and holding my crying infant brother on her hip while my 4-year-old brother stands next to her. I find it remarkable that as a single parent she was able to raise three boys and support us in endeavors like motocross and hockey. As her oldest son, I quickly learned how to find my own way, and I was always looking out for my younger brothers.

When I was 12 years old, I decided I should start to shave my face. It was more about the rite of passage into manhood, and less about the need to rid myself of a few hairs. I proudly walked to a convenience store and used my own money to buy shaving cream and disposable razors. Soon I was shaving my face regularly, and my brother, who was 10, became interested. Naturally I passed on my technique as if I were an old pro, and in no time, we were shaving our nearly hairless faces together.

I have always taken great pride in being able to teach my younger brothers things I learned on my own. This drive extends into many other parts of my life as well. When I was a college student approaching graduation, I faced a trail-blazing moment: finding a job. I knew I wanted to work in finance, but getting there was a different story. The guys I worked road construction with during my college summers would tease I was off to become a lawyer, the epitome of white-collar jobs, drawing laughs from the crew. The pressure was intense, and my parents were not much help in the job search process. My mom is a paralegal who moonlights nights and weekends at a FedEx shipping center, and my stepfather works in law enforcement. There were only a handful of investment banking jobs available on my campus, for which the competition was fierce. I ultimately sourced my own investment banking job through cold calling. I reached out to over 50 bankers and HR representatives before I finally secured my dream job at [Investment Bank].

Now, through my undergraduate school's mentorship program, I connect with undergraduate students seeking career advice related to investment banking. As with my younger brothers, I love being able to leverage my hard-won experience to help others, particularly with the stressful investment banking recruiting process. After I worked with one student for over two years on his resume and interview preparation, he landed his dream job with [Investment Bank]. It was incredibly empowering for me to help someone else secure a job I had been rejected for just a couple of years earlier. I suddenly realized the impact I could have on other people's lives by sharing my own experiences.

At [my firm], our team was lean. The associate who I reported to and I were the only junior bankers supporting four Managing Directors. Six months into my time on the job, the associate left. I was petrified. My team was too small to have a formal training program, and there was so much I had yet to learn from him. I was able to get through this rough spot simply by taking one day at a time. When a topic came up that I wasn't comfortable with, I would work through it using resources I could find online, leveraging friends I had at other banks, and even calling the S&P Capital IQ help line. During this time I was able to single-handedly support four successful transactions worth over $400 million in aggregate value.

A few months later when the firm hired a new analyst, I was the one training him! It was less than a year after I had started with the firm, but I had already taught myself everything I needed to know. Much like with my younger brothers, I took great pride in passing on the knowledge I had gained. My challenging experience made me a better teacher, and in some ways, I had already developed my own training curriculum. I knew which lessons I should teach up front, and which ones I should let him figure out for himself. It gave me great pride to learn he was promoted to associate a couple years later.

My decision to leave [the investment bank] to focus on the health care sector was not easy. We were a small, tight-knit group, and I had developed strong relationships with the Managing Directors. However, I knew in my gut I was making the right move. Joining [Life Science Venture Capital Firm] gave me the opportunity to work on tremendously impactful problems in health care, such as diabetes prevention and chronic pain management, while leveraging my finance and entrepreneurial skills.

My most significant experience has been leading the development of a pitch for a new behavioral health business. This was an enormously ambiguous project. I had built many financial models before, but only for existing businesses. Building a new financial model from scratch required me to design much of the clinical and operating models for the business first. My years of teaching myself and finding my own way came in remarkably handy. I started by interviewing the experts: psychiatrists, psychologists, primary care physicians, and consumers. I then looked closely at other companies and tried to apply best practices from their operating models to my own. All the while I documented the logic behind my assumptions in detail.

When the time came to pitch the idea to the President of [the firm], I was quite anxious. I was responsible for guiding him and the rest of our investment team through my research, assumptions, and financial projections. Ultimately, the project was approved for $11 million of seed funding. [The President] congratulated me and then requested my financial framework be used as a template for all new investment ideas going forward.

From teaching my younger brother to shave to developing a best practice at a $250 billion health care company, I have always found the most rewarding part of any achievement, no matter how big or small, to be the part where I get to turn around and share my lessons learned with others. I plan to continue charting my own course in life. In fact, it is the only way I know. But what excites me most is the opportunity to share my learnings with others.

ANALYSIS

Clayton writes an inspirational and relatable essay where he describes how being the oldest child in a single-parent household has taught him to both be quick to learn and teach others. His essay opens up with a description of his family portrait of himself, his mom, and two younger brothers that allows the reader to imagine Clayton's family and connect with him. This hook also establishes his identity as a self-taught mentor figure for others, which he elaborates on later and applies to his career in finance.

To introduce this concept, Clayton recalls experiences passing down knowledge to his younger brothers about shaving and college. He goes on to explain how in his own pursuit of a career in finance he needed to pave the way for himself.

Clayton again ties in the theme of self-teaching and eventually advising and mentoring newer associates while working at the investment bank before transitioning to his current career, where he talks about how he used those learning experiences to work on a highly successful pitch. This is where he truly reframes this role from something in his personal identity to an asset that he can employ in business. It shows his creativity and adaptability, merging Clayton's background with his professional goals to create a more holistic picture of him.

Clayton continues to weave the notion of self-teaching and then teaching others throughout his story: whether it was shaving or his achievements in venture capital. In his conclusion, he zooms out to indicate to the admissions officers that his greater goals in life are beyond business or finance. In fact, it is his dedication to teaching and his passion for learning and helping others that expresses to the admissions officers the impact that he will have with an MBA as well as the humility he will bring to the class at the university.

—Isabella Tran

Leonardo L.

Home State/Country: California, USA
Undergraduate School: Stanford University
GPA Range: 3.3–3.7
GRE: 307 T (151Q; 156V)
Work Experience: Corporate Finance
Word Count: 900

ESSAY

What matters to me most in life is transforming seemingly negative circumstances into positive learning opportunities. During certain phases of my life, I have been homeless, lacked parental assistance, experienced being undocumented, and almost gave up my dream to attend college. But, thanks to the support of my community and my grandmother's lessons, I have become one of the most resourceful and tenacious people in the world. The fact that I am applying to one of the most selective business schools in the country makes my heart burst with triumph and this application serves as a personal reminder of my potential.

I believe that I can change the world by inspiring others to continue their dreams and by demonstrating how perseverance and humility can lead to great outcomes. I also believe that my experiences will be beneficial to anyone who considers giving up their dreams. When I was a High School student, I worked at a Latino grocery store. One day, I met two fellow Mexican immigrants talking about their entrepreneurial goals, and I still remember how their eyes glimmered with hope and optimism. However, another man interrupted their conversation by foretelling that if he "could not get a business loan because his English was not good enough to talk to the banks" then they would be rejected as well. At that point in life, I was also facing a language barrier, but I never allowed external influences to deviate my path. That day I promised myself that I would never allow my background to become a Scarlet Letter, but rather raise a shining beacon for the Hispanic community.

When I immigrated to the US about ten years ago, I did not speak English and at first everything sounded like a cacophony. To some, I was both an outsider and a foe simply for existing. Despite my deficiencies, I attended school devotedly, and earned top honors every year, even when certain people continually told me to quit school and "start working" in the sweltering Florida fields. When I felt the urge to give up my dreams, I recited my grandmother's proverbs about how "everything in life has a solution, except death, which is unavoidable," and kept fighting with courage. Thanks to my grades, community impact, and test scores, I was granted admission to the undergraduate programs at Stanford and Harvard. Now, I am on my way to building a better future for my family to finally exit a cycle of poverty and to savor the fruits of my hard work.

Yet, each time that I learn and improve, I never self-attribute my success, and I thank the people and institutions that believed in me and encouraged my dreams. From working at a nonprofit group that supports homeless and low-income students, to my professors and my alma mater, my supporters have cemented the values that I respect. In this great nation, I have learned that the unity of purpose and the humility to ask for help allow you to succeed and that the best kind of success is when you realize that passion overcomes present limitations. I want to become a voice for the marginalized and an example of how one can succeed despite facing several setbacks. I want others to know that failure in the present does not efface our intrinsic ability to succeed, like how this country has faced great depressions to later regain economic rejuvenation. America is not only a land of immigrants; it is a land of dreams on which each soul plants the concept of a better future. A land where that seed grows into a tree of accomplishments and happiness. Drought comes, but it does not efface the hope for progress. It is a dimension where time vanishes with the continual regeneration of forgotten ideas: A haven where differences disappear with the union of purpose. I came here to be a leader and to build a better future and I want my story to be the source and the reason for people to believe in the American Dream. Even if invisible lines divide us, we will always be one human race, one body, one heart.

Above all, I would like to use the power of business to start a social enterprise and influence society to protect vulnerable students and children. By providing ample support and technical accessibility, I deeply believe that students from low-income backgrounds can gain a stronger set of skills and participate actively in the economy. If it were not for my middle school mentors, I would have never learned how to use Excel or Word. As such, I want to replicate this experience and design a social network to connect mentors and educators with low-income and homeless students.

Hence, I hope that HBS will give me the tools and connections to amplify my vision, inspire others through leadership, and support my nonprofit. I would like to start working on my start-up idea immediately and that is why I am requesting deferred admission. In the following years, I will commence my own research process to prepare my business acumen and design a scalable solution that will bridge the gap between my capabilities and my edtech start-up goals. My biggest task will be to bring education opportunities to marginalized communities and use the power of technology ethically to galvanize this dream. Thank you so much for considering my application.

Sincerely, Leonardo L.

ANALYSIS

Written with passion, Leonardo's personal statement reveals how resilience and hope guide his pursuit of academic and entrepreneurial success. His intimate narrative opens with a simple articulation of an age-old mantra: with hardship comes opportunity for growth. Leonardo establishes how his encounters with impoverishment, parental neglect, and undocumentation compelled him to grow more resourceful and resolute. He also attributes his personal success to networks of community support he received in times of hardship.

Leonardo then delves into a conversation about his experience as an American immigrant, a difficult adjustment characterized by language barriers and vitriolic social attitudes. Through honest reflections, he recalls how he was nearly deterred from seeking higher education. He recalls being urged by peers to prioritize work above high school. As these mounting social pressures stacked up against Leonardo, his grandmother—a figure mentioned several times throughout the narrative—offered him both reassurance and advice. Encouraged by her proverbs, Leonardo continued studying diligently. In the face of socioeconomic hardship, he embraced an optimistic outlook, pursued higher education, and emerged triumphant. By demonstrating that resilience and motivation can, indeed, prevail over socioeconomic constraints, Leonardo hopes that underprivileged students can look to his example and be reminded that even the wildest of dreams are attainable with persistent effort.

Towards the end, Leonardo draws parallels between his personal growth and the evolution of America. He shares that failure, on a national or personal scale, is not fatal and can, instead, inspire improvement. He hopes to pave a path forward for underprivileged children by creating a network to help educators get in touch with homeless and low-income students.

His personal narrative echoes the importance of embracing adversity as a vehicle for progress and self-growth. Having experienced and overcome socioeconomic hurdles to arrive at this point in his academic success, he funnels his newfound entrepreneurial knowledge into giving back and offering underprivileged students more educational opportunities.

—Chelsea Hu

ANAND G.

Home State/Country: India
Undergraduate School: University of Maryland
GPA Range: 3.3–3.7
GMAT: 740 T (42V; 48Q)
Work Experience: Renewable Energy
Word Count: 1,394

ESSAY

In August 2017, a year into my Associate-level role at [Indian Renewable Energy Company], I found a great acquisition target for my company. My thinking was that the target company's digital energy efficiency product offering would complement our existing portfolio well and serve as a future growth engine. Wanting to respect institutional hierarchy, I initially introduced the target company to a couple of my senior colleagues—P&L owners at the firm—who framed the acquisition rationale differently than what I had hypothesized. They wanted to use the target company's tech stack on our existing renewable energy assets and not necessarily build on its existing product line. The investment committee (IC) wasn't too impressed with the proposal we put together. I didn't take the IC's lackluster response at face value, however. On a visit to the US in November 2017, while accompanying my CEO as the lead planner for a separate market research exercise there, I brought it up with him on one of our car rides. I told him the start-up had experienced founders, a working digital energy efficiency product, consistent year-on-year growth in revenues, creditworthy customers, and sound unit economics, and that it made sense to explore an acquisition for these reasons. He listened and said I should make another proposal to the IC once we got back to India. As it turned out, my CEO and the IC loved the strategic thinking and the overall opportunity, and we ended up offering a $5 million deal to this company. More importantly, though, I earned the internal political capital to develop the firm's first-of-its-kind early-stage corporate development practice.

This experience defines me. I have an ability to find value accretive, unique opportunities, with a laser-focus on combating climate change. My journey started in high school. When I was sixteen, I watched workers in Pune, my hometown in India, burn tar in the open air to create liquid asphalt to lay on a road. I had a visceral reaction as I watched, and I later discovered the invisible effects of the emissions were even more alarming. Determined to do something to help the environment, I founded a social enterprise that planted over 2,000 trees in the city. I then built on an unconventional opening. I visited the United Nations India office and mounted a persistent campaign, leveraging my social entrepreneurship work, to get involved at the global level. After multiple applications and interview rounds, the U.N. did endorse me. They named me India's official junior ambassador to the COP15 climate change negotiation talks in Copenhagen. I spent the entire flight to Denmark strategizing what I'd say to the US President. As these things go, I didn't manage an audience with President Obama, but I did meet a Professor of Environmental Economics from the University of Maryland who encouraged me to apply to the school for its undergraduate studies program and offered financial assistance if I got accepted. I did, and that is how things ended up unfolding. I started as a typical foreigner in America—I had no family or friends when I landed—but over three and a half years of college, I began to fondly call Maryland home. (I even became a Ravens fan.)

Towards the end of my sophomore year, I became slightly bewildered about confronting the job market. I had few connections in the professional world, a niche undergraduate degree, and an immigrant visa status—I was also on course to graduating ahead of my class, so I had those many fewer months to find a job. Against this backdrop, I mounted a campaign of over fifty informational interviews for an aerial survey of the local energy industry. Through this effort, I landed a position in the arcane but impactful energy efficiency retrofit industry that helps everyday Americans slash their carbon footprint by retrofitting their homes and businesses with energy-saving technologies. In my first job, I led over half a million dollars of energy efficiency retrofits. At my second job, at [Consulting Firm], beyond my day-to-day analyst-level responsibilities, I identified a niche market for designing energy efficiency incentive programs for city governments. I built consensus among the leadership in my business unit that this was a market worth going after. I, then, led the preparation of various competitive proposals, and we went on to win a consulting project for the City of Cambridge in Massachusetts (home of the HBS!).

The boldest move in my career, however, wasn't the move to America, but the move back from the USA to India. I'd grown comfortable in my energy efficiency niche, and the road to a green card beckoned. Yet the dual prospect of riding the clean energy wave and solving the critical problem of climate change from the frontlines of where it matters the most pulled me back to my home country. I was able to find a role in the best company in the field in India, under the best person leading the charge. Climate change is going to test the limits of modern society. Gurugram, India, where I live, is dangerously close to running out of drinking water and is the world's most polluted city. I have faced instances where I haven't had access to clean drinking water at my home for forty-eight-hour periods at a stretch. I have frequently fallen ill in my last three years here due to the severity of the air pollution problem. I also don't dare to step out of air-conditioned environments during daytime in the summers, as we have experienced record heatwaves and temperatures in recent years. If as someone presumably in the top quartile of the population I have experienced the brutality firsthand, one can only imagine how the rest of my compatriots will suffer as the crisis intensifies. And it's crippling our economy as well. The World Bank estimates that climate-related calamities will eat away a minimum of 250 basis points off India's annual GDP growth going forward. At my job at [Renewable Energy Company] in India, I saw that our profit margins were shrinking as competition in the sector was intensifying. Companies like ours with substantial free cash projections on the back of existing projects need to find new growth areas to deploy that cash effectively, five to ten years down the line. So, as I developed our early-stage investing and corporate development operation, I traveled to incubators and conferences around the world and built a robust deal flow of opportunities for the company. Particularly in India, I have been inspired by entrepreneurs building a range of cleantech products and services suited for the country such as new inverters, automated energy efficiency solutions, emissions control devices, smart weather forecasting tools, grid integration tools, electric vehicles, energy storage, and many others. The work I've done in setting up this network will not only help the company hedge itself against the risk of market stagnation but also unlock a larger pool of economic value in the climate mitigation domain.

I now have clarity on my long-term goal: to start my own VC fund devoted to confronting climate change in the developing world. I plan to tap the network of opportunities I've stitched to-gether in India and elsewhere and source investment and strategic guidance to foster these young enterprises. Studying at the HBS will give me the remaining tools I need to accomplish this goal. In-side the classroom, for example, I am looking forward to learning from one of the most renowned investors in the world in the class on "Investing—Risk, Return & Impact." Outside the classroom, I will immerse myself in the energy and India clubs to host events on campus that bring together luminaries across academia, industry, and policy circles. I am also excited to get involved with and apply to the Rock Venture Partners program to gain practical VC expe-rience; given my expertise advising cleantech start-ups in India, I am eager to add value to the Rock Accelerator teams as part of the program. Climate change mitigation needs our attention—and capi-tal—in the next four to five decades. It is perhaps the most important problem of our time. A business education from HBS will help me catalyze my efforts in finding, nurturing, and commercializing clean-tech companies that can help decarbonize our society and create eco-nomic value in the process.

ANALYSIS

In this retrospective essay, Anand interweaves his lifelong ambi-tion of tackling climate change and his appreciation for business as a tool to realize this ambition. Anand introduces this "the-sis" with a hook that sets the scene for a transformative experience during his employment in a renewable energy company. While his hook creates anticipation, the rest of the anecdote subtly highlights Anand's key characteristics such as creativity and perseverance.

Anand demonstrates the depth of his passion for climate change in the essay's body by describing his journey to become "India's official junior ambassador to the COP15." The narration not only provides ample evidence of adamant focus to tackle problems through powerful diction like "visceral reaction" but also illuminates the admirable steps Anand took to forge his career path.

Later, Anand displays his flair for considering both the economic and human aspects of the climate change problem; he is simultaneously concerned with both "the rest of [his] compatriots" and India's GDP. This demonstration of a valuable leadership skill emphasizes Anand's readiness for Harvard Business School to the reader.

By referencing specific classes and programs available at Harvard Business School, Anand successfully both exhibits a great interest in the school and states how he will use this education to better the world in his conclusion. The essay maintains a strong focus on Anand's desire to tackle climate change using business. This allows Anand to showcase his suitable characteristics to HBS: from his ability to empathize to his ability to spot "a great acquisition target."

—Ece Hasdemir

Miguel C.

Home State/Country: Brazil
Undergraduate School: Federal University of Rio Grande do Sul
GPA Range: 3.7–4.0
GMAT: 700 T (38V; 49Q)
Work Experience: Private Equity
Word Count: 1,376

ESSAY

Business executives, entrepreneurs, community and rising leaders—over 2,000 attendees filled the convention hall, voices echoing loudly. Another 65,000+ joined online, waiting for the Leadership Development Institute Forum to start. It was November 2017, and I was about to address the audience with my speech. As I walked toward the stage, I thought of how fulfilled I felt by the event, and remembered my mother's words, which had framed all my efforts to get there: "You're not here by chance. Make an impact wherever you go."

I was born in Cruz Alta (High Cross), a tiny city in southern Brazil. The son of a farming family, I grew up with a passion for all things agricultural, especially horses. But I longed to know more about the world beyond our farm, reading news magazines a week after they came out, due to our remoteness. I was especially inspired by stories of leaders like Fernando Henrique Cardoso (former president who drove large positive change) and Gustavo Franco (former Finance minister who solved our inflation problem). Their stories—

and my mother's words—inspired me to pursue a larger purpose: becoming a true agent of change while helping others—especially young people—do the same. I knew I had to learn from these inspirational leaders. Achieving that meant leaving the comfort of Cruz Alta. "I think I have to go," I told my parents at age 14—a rare statement in a country where most young people live at home into their mid-20s. Though stunned initially, my parents knew I had large-scale ambitions and supported my plan. Their belief in me only increased my conviction. I moved to live and attend school in Porto Alegre, the state capital. I missed home but embraced my new life. I studied hard and took up tennis, determined to build skill and compete against those who'd already been playing for 10+ years. I did, performing capably while learning to lose with grace. Ultimately a heel injury stopped me, but I'd gained a strong sense of determination from the sport. The bright spot of my departure from tennis: I could focus fully on my vision. Through hard work I won admission to Federal University of Rio Grande do Sul, one of Brazil's best. My growing network there led to meeting influential businessman Jorge Gerdau, who spoke of the "leadership gap" Brazil suffered. His words reinforced my desire to foster young people's potential, creating a multiplier effect.

My ambition to continue learning from inspiring leaders took me to São Paulo, Brazil's "hub of impact." I joined the competitive [Brazilian Investment Bank] Trainee Program, knowing that being in a renowned financial institution would enhance my analytical/people skills and quickly increase my exposure to Brazilian leaders of impact. As an RM, I've moved closer to my childhood inspiration: I interact daily with owners and C-level executives of large Brazilian companies, learning from them while guiding them through Brazil's worst-ever political, economic, and social crisis. Business, I've recognized, is a powerful social change engine. For example, I helped finance the expansion of a real estate client building affordable housing for 1000+ low-income people in a Southern city, creating large employment and housing opportunities.

Alongside this work I've been happy to serve as a mentor for the same Young Leadership Program I'd benefited from, guiding five rising talents on their careers/dreams and identifying their development areas. For example, last year, when my mentee said she felt unfulfilled, I helped her create a "career map" and approach her manager about new responsibilities; she's now performing well and won a recent promotion. My efforts to develop the next generation have been even larger beyond the bank's walls. Since 2013 I've been part of [Brazilian Nonprofit Organization], fostering entrepreneurship and young leaders through projects and lectures with renowned leaders including Jorge Paulo Lemann, a Brazilian businessman and advocate of social impact. I joined the Institute as a volunteer, spending two years in a rigorous training program; the best moments were learning directly from diverse leaders, such as late nights discussing potential solutions to Brazil's toughest challenges: education, infrastructure, corruption, etc. In 2016, I was elected Director of Membership Development and reformulated all members' training with inclusion of vital topics such as impact investing, attracting even more members. I motivated them through training/mentorship, created a lecture series about driving impact through entrepreneurship, and got our message out to a broader audience by co-writing an entrepreneurship book that sold 10,000+ copies. Based on my dedication, the board asked me to become its president in 2017.

It hasn't always been easy managing my growing roles at

[Investment Bank] and [Nonprofit Organization]. But I've embraced and grown from each. For example, I've learned so much managing [Nonprofit Organization]'s five-director board, all of them much more experienced than I am. Under my guidance, the 100-member institute has led/expanded projects such as providing entrepreneurship classes to children and developing young leaders in São Paulo's most disadvantaged communities. Our efforts crystallized with the [Nonprofit Organization] Forum we organized last November with leaders including Brazilian heads of Amazon, Uber, Google, and Santander. They were to speak to the large audience about entrepreneurship and new technology. Through broad, network-driven promotion, within two weeks we sold all 2,000 tickets, and I secured a sponsor to live-stream the Forum for free, to reach a broader audience (65,000+ ultimately joined the audience this way). Preparing to address everyone as opening speaker that night, I felt only excitement. "Through strong leadership and new technology, we can change Brazil's status quo!" I said as I took the stage. The crowd voiced their approval. It was a sign we were on the right path.

This year, as [a Nonprofit Organization] Board Member, I've been happy to meet with young talents and hear of the growing impact they've had. Indeed, our members have driven positive change for multinationals, family businesses, political offices, and the broad community. My goal now is to launch [Nonprofit Organization] branches in five other Brazilian capital cities to make our impact widespread. My role at [Nonprofit Organization] led to an invitation to join the Legacy for Brazilian Youth program created by former president Fernando Henrique Cardoso, who'd inspired me from an early age. Here was a new opportunity to work and learn with great talents. Recently, Cardoso and other program leaders chose my team's project for scaling and implementation: we are studying developed countries' education models for mentoring and fostering young talent, and will create policy recommendations to deliver to Brazil's new president after the November election.

These experiences have galvanized my desire to make a difference, and to integrate my professional vision with that of social impact. Our most critical imperative, I believe, is to improve our education system to develop next-generation leaders who can guide Brazil to a brighter future. As such, post-HBS I plan to integrate the financial analysis and deal-structuring skills I've gained at [Investment Bank] with my [Nonprofit Organization] and Legacy program experience to join an education company that is consolidating opportunities in the sector. I've recently spoken to the CEO of Bahema, a venture that acquires and operates schools, investing in a new education system. He is excited about my experience and vision. My long-term ambition is to drive a large impact by leading an innovative education organization that fosters the potential of our young citizens and future leaders. I also intend to serve on nonprofit boards of new ventures/initiatives in this sector, to direct investments to high-level education projects. To achieve my vision, I need to enhance my knowledge, capabilities, and network. A campus visit last year and conversations with [HBS Alum] '18 and [HBS Alum] '13 highlighted that HBS has the best resources to help me grow: general management training, unparalleled opportunities for innovation and entrepreneurship, and a sharp focus on developing leaders of impact. The Social Enterprise Initiative, for example, can yield critical knowledge, insights, and experiences, and I'll learn from my visionary classmates while sharing my ideas and contributing to the community. My mother was right: We are not here by chance, but to make an impact. With my determination and the help of HBS, this son of Cruz Alta will give everything to drive a large-scale impact in coming years.

ANALYSIS

In Miguel's impactful narrative, he showcases his personal growth and past accomplishments to demonstrate his passion for helping Brazil's youth and low-income citizens. Miguel sets the scene by describing the leadership organization's forum, where he remembered his mother saying, "You're not here by chance. Make an impact wherever you go." This phrase sets the tone and structures the narrative he wants HBS admissions to consider.

The body paragraphs follow Miguel's theme of being determined to make an impact wherever he goes, no matter the difficulty. He explains how he took up tennis and learned how to win and lose gracefully, highlighting some of his personality traits: confidence and resilience. Similarly, instead of showing bitterness towards an injury that prevented him from playing tennis, Miguel refocuses his attention on tasks that would make more of an impact in his community. Miguel shows his commitment to helping Brazil's youth by using his past knowledge to help aspiring Brazilian kids. He describes the difficulty of balancing his work with two organizations, especially since he manages a board of directors more experienced than he is. His well-written paragraphs show how he has gotten involved in his community, rather than simply telling the admissions officers.

Towards the end, Miguel ties his experiences to the overarching theme of living up to his mother's phrase, realizing his life's purpose of providing Brazil's youth with the resources and education to succeed. Miguel goes on to describe how an HBS MBA will provide him with the opportunity to work with a company that is investing in a new education system.

—Sofia Diaz-Rodriguez

HUNTER G.

Home State/Country: Indiana, USA
Undergraduate School: DePauw University
GPA Range: 3.3–3.7
GMAT: 710 T (45V; 43Q)
Work Experience: Pharmaceuticals
Word Count: 1,230

ESSAY

I don't remember much from when I was six years old, but one memory comes easily to mind. I had just finished taking a bath, and I remember standing on the tile naked and confused as my mom struggled to tell me why my dad wouldn't be home that night. Earlier that day—she choked out through sobs—he suffered a heart attack at the gym. He died at the hospital shortly after. He was 39 years old.

I wish I could say this was an isolated incident, but my family has been shaken again and again by premature deaths related to heart disease, Alzheimer's Disease and complications from obesity and diabetes. These health issues are all too common, especially among lower classes and rural communities in the Midwest. Having grown up visiting family in the depressed former steel capital of Gary and in the isolated farm town of Winamac, Indiana, I am intimately familiar with the devastating effects of chronic diseases and the broad unawareness of their causes among the general public. Like my grandmother, who had no idea that daily biscuits and pie can lead to chronic inflammation and insulin resistance, people are misled or simply unaware of the aspects of their lifestyle that are killing them. I am passionate about ending this tragedy, and I saw an opportunity to help by joining [Pharmaceutical Company].

I've spent my professional career building brands that treat inflammatory diseases. In one of many market research experiences, I found myself sitting behind a one-way mirror at a facility in Boston, observing interviews with Crohn's Disease patients on the other side. One patient, when asked how her disease impacts her life, confided, "I'm not the mother for my kids that I want to be." She described how pain and fatigue from her disease keeps her watching from the sidelines as her kids play and grow.

Having grown up in a single-parent household, I know the fear and tension she feels about leaving a void in her children's lives. In my current role, being able to empathize with patients has helped me build richness into our brand strategy and distill insights for shared understanding among my marketing and non-marketing colleagues alike. I've helped the team understand the specific ways in which relieving destructive symptoms helps people live more fully, achieve more and be more present.

I am grateful that my work at [the pharmaceutical company] helps restore patients' lives. However, after four years of experience across three brands and six diseases, I believe there is so much more we can do. Today, we treat some of the most devastating diseases with "Band-Aids." Even best-in-class medicines do not solve underlying problems; they just make patients feel better for a time. What many consider innovation in fact represents incremental progress, with new medicines offering modest gains in efficacy over existing treatments. Innovation should aim to alter the course of disease or eliminate it altogether.

Achieving true step changes in chronic disease treatment requires transformative leadership—the ability to understand the essence of a problem and see an unconventional path to solving it. Pharma leaders consistently make high-stakes decisions: between internal investment or external innovation, among assets going to clinical trials on limited R&D budgets, and on the clinical trial endpoints—how we measure success—given high hurdles for regulatory and statistical rigor. Each is an opportunity to stretch further. We need bold leaders who can navigate the complexities of the health care landscape and who have the empathy, courage and decision-making capabilities to place big bets.

I am pursuing an MBA to develop these skills, the confidence to make trade-off decisions in the face of imperfect data and the judgment to allocate finite resources with greatest possible impact—attributes HBS' case method is uniquely suited to hone. When I return to [the pharmaceutical company] and take on greater leadership roles, I will use these skills to identify novel ways of connecting science to patient outcomes and push the organization to be more aspirational in our pursuit of medical innovation.

I know HBS is the perfect place to pursue this mission because the resources of the Health Care Initiative, the more than 20 faculty members dedicated to health care research, and topical courses like Innovating in Health Care and Commercializing Science offer unparalleled access to the forefront of health care innovation. In addition, the robust Health Care Club, with more than 250 members and many mentorship opportunities, provides a diverse, talented network primed to help me revolutionize the paradigm of chronic disease treatment.

As passionate as I am about HBS' resources and alignment with my goals, I am equally excited by the students' commitment to supporting one another and making a difference in their communities. This became evident to me in stories like Kevin Ferguson's shared on the *We Are HBS* podcast, and it was reinforced when I visited campus. Being raised by a single working mother, engaged communities played a central role in my development, and I seek out environments where people invest in one another's success. Despite being devastated by the loss of my dad, my mom did everything in her power to provide us with stability and opportunity—from her 35-year career as a hygienist in the same dental office to her choice not to remarry. Of her many reactions, perhaps the most impactful was her determination to surround us with nurturing communities where we could thrive. That's how we ended up in the Immaculate Heart of Mary neighborhood, where everything from Sunday night pitch-ins to the local Boy Scout Troop seemed tailor-made to support my single mother as she strove to raise two young kids. Boy Scouts, for instance, taught me skills I would not have gotten at home, like first aid and fire-building. More importantly, I learned how to lead and what it means to be a man of character. This community and others like it filled gaps that I felt growing up without a father.

I see Harvard's engaged, passionate community as a natural fit, and I am excited to contribute. I would relish the opportunity to lead within the Health Care Club, specifically the Biotech and Pharma interest group, and organize the annual health care conference with a focus on defining true innovation in chronic disease treatment. I would also be thrilled to produce *We Are HBS*, which motivated my passion for the school before I ever visited Boston. I have grown the most when I share myself with the people and organizations around me, and I look forward to bringing this attitude of reciprocal investment to HBS.

As you consider my application, I want you to know that I have a unique appreciation for the role communities can play in the development of people, and for the unique role leaders can play in shaping a community. I want you to know that I've suffered a great deal of loss at the hands of a deficient health care system, and I'm determined to prevent the same tragedy for others. I want you to see that I've spent four years not just building brands and creating experiences for chronically ill patients, but also learning about the system and preparing myself to improve it. And I want you to share in my conviction that these things together make HBS the best next step in my journey.

ANALYSIS

Hunter opens his essay with an impactful anecdote about his father's untimely passing and how Hunter has witnessed similar deaths in his family. He goes on to note that chronic health issues are common in the rural, lower-income communities he is familiar with. Eventually, his determination to confront this issue drives him to join the pharmaceutical industry. Apart from serving as an engaging hook, this introduction also frames Hunter as someone who deeply values kinship and community.

In the body of the essay, Hunter details how his experiences in the pharmaceuticals industry led him to realize the limitations of current treatments, as well as his desire to improve them. Here Hunter introduces his main motivation for applying to Harvard Business School: to gain the requisite leadership and judgment skills for him to pursue this endeavor. He also explains why HBS's program is the right fit for him by mentioning specific health care–related resources and initiatives. As such, Hunter is able to clearly show how an MBA can help him positively impact the pharmaceutical industry.

Finally, Hunter explains that he chose Harvard Business School because of its vibrant campus culture, which he finds reminiscent of the close-knit communities he grew up with. In addition, he also outlines ways he can contribute to HBS's inclusive and support-ive environment. This effectively showcases Hunter as a passionate leader and a deserving MBA candidate, further affirming his suit-ability for HBS.

—Alison Tan

TIM C.

Home State/Country: California, USA
Undergraduate School: University of Pennsylvania
GPA Range: 3.7–4.0
GMAT: 760 T (50V; 46Q)
Work Experience: Consulting
Word Count: 911

ESSAY

It was in the last week of my externship at [Transportation Start-up] when over 300 employees (two-thirds of the company) were laid off, including nearly everyone I'd worked with for six months. I was shocked by the sudden turn of events. They were the leading transportation start-up in Bangladesh but had just failed to secure a Series B investment. Frustratingly, the downsizing had little to do with how well [the start-up] performed and more to do with the disappointing IPOs of two tech giants across the world—Uber and Lyft. Here I saw the very real limitations of capital not flowing into companies and countries where I felt needed it most—where it could have the largest societal impact per dollar invested. I want to lead the charge to get more capital into the geographies, industries, and companies where the potential of impact on underserved people is optimized.

I attribute my global empathy and fascination with the world to growing up with a giant world map on our living room wall pinned with photos of family friends living all over the world. As Christian missionaries, my parents visited and befriended people of all nationalities and brought home stories of people they had served. They modeled for me the profound impact one could have on another's life, from providing a struggling mother with food to feed her family to giving love and hope to an orphan child. Expecting to follow in my parents' footsteps and become a missionary, I went on numerous service trips to developing countries like Paraguay and the Philippines where I taught English and helped build schools. I gained perspective and connection to people in environments different from my own but realized that the inequality was far greater than I could effectively reduce through a direct one-on-one model.

While in college, I saw my two older brothers thriving in the world of finance, which introduced me to another model for societal impact: be successful and use your financial resources for good. To learn more, I did summer internships at a tech start-up and, enjoying the experience, joined a for-profit consulting firm after college. At [the firm], I first understood how capital had both the scale and the influence to drive impact. Based on our analyses, our private equity clients would shift hundreds of millions of dollars in and out of markets, which would have meaningful effects on the business' surrounding communities. But often the work didn't align with my core values of serving the underserved. As I contemplated next steps, I kept returning to a question my brothers had asked me—"what would you regret not doing when you look back at your life in fifty years?"

That question led me to join [Social Impact Consulting Group] where I could continue to sharpen my business skills while working on creating change at scale on social issues. My first project was advising the $2 billion [Impact Fund] on making impact-minded investments. Though they clearly had financial know-how, [the firm] needed guidance in measuring impact using data-driven methods and incorporating it into their investment framework. My role was, as [the firm] described it, to be an "impact bodyguard." For example, when I worked on their $150 million investment into [a microfinance institution focused on the rural market], we directed them to include impact covenants to ensure that a portion of their loans would go to low-income, rural farmers that didn't have prior access to financing. I realized that there was a giant gap of expertise and knowledge in being a true "impact" investor, not just an investor that happens to have social impact.

Though I conceptually understood the social impact of my work, wanting to see the impact actualized on the ground, I searched for high-growth, impact-focused companies, which is how I ended up at [the transportation start-up]. There, I saw the positive impact on the more than 50,000 drivers who now made living wages, and on the 3,000,000 riders whose commutes were cut in half. Moreover, the positive effect of impact investing capital in [the start-up] was validated when I represented them at the National Economic Mobility Roundtable hosted by a leading NGO, BRAC. High ranking government officials and national nonprofit leaders looked to me to describe the social and economic impact [the start-up] and other private sector companies have had on low-income individuals through creating quality jobs at scale. My experience at [the start-up] has confirmed my belief in the role that impact investing could have on individuals, communities, and even entire countries. However, it was also at [the start-up] where I saw the profit-driven constraints of the investors as demonstrated by the financially-motivated downsizing I experienced.

During and after HBS, I will push the impact investing industry to become more impact-first and globally-focused. While working at leading impact, I will construct creative solutions like impact bonds and global fund management structures to further advance their thinking and actions. I envision promoting additional accountability around manager compensation, incorporating predictive impact modeling, and utilizing global sourcing as commonplace practices in these funds. I will bring a bipartisan perspective from both the for profit and nonprofit world, international experience, and knowledge from within ventures and with investors to lead and innovate impact investing.

In my living room one day, I envision an even bigger world map, now even more crowded with faces of people I helped. I hope to help make the world a more equitable place by moving capital, at scale, to those who need it most in the world.

ANALYSIS

Embodying the virtues of a global scholar and a social entrepreneur, Tim's insightful narrative reveals how elements of his upbringing continue to underlie his pursuit of corporate stewardship. A son of two missionaries, Tim espouses his parents' culturally rich worldview and qualities of generosity and compassion by harnessing his own entrepreneurial wisdom as a means to ameliorate the conditions of the globally underserved.

Tim begins by depicting the experience of corporate downsizing all too familiar for businesses left in the dust of sweeping market globalization. Tim recalls the distress facing hundreds of employees at the budding transportation enterprise, whose prospects of growth were hindered severely by the entrance of Lyft and Uber into the Bangladeshi market. While lamentable, the corporate contraption Tim witnessed reminded him of the stark wealth disparities that mark the twenty-first-century global landscape, urging him to leverage his financial expertise to introduce capital to economically deprived communities.

Later, Tim entered the world of finance, viewing the finance sector as a bastion of opportunity, not only to enhance his own career prospects but also to contribute towards community development. He then joined a consulting group as an "impact bodyguard," tasked with measuring the social impact of corporate actions and reporting back to the firm with recommendations surrounding community outreach.

Tim reveals the milestones he hopes to achieve as a young entrepreneur. He pledges to approach his upcoming projects with an unfaltering focus on community well-being. Rather than betraying his virtues and chasing solely career prospects, Tim remains loyal to the aspiration of effective altruism that has inspired visionaries to contribute towards the greater good.

—Chelsea Hu

Lailah T.

Home State/Country: New York, USA
Undergraduate School: Worcester Polytechnic Institute
GPA Range: 3.7–4.0
GRE: 308 T (154V; 154Q)
Work Experience: Manufacturing
Word Count: 1,008

ESSAY

It was March 23. Stuck in South America for the next five weeks with only two days' worth of clothes, no Lactaid pills, a broken phone, and a broken laptop. I was the definition of Murphy's Law. My time in Paraguay has been one of the most interesting experiences ever. From trouble at the airport where I could not check in my luggage and thus was only allowed to bring carry-on with me, to breaking my phone the very first week of arrival, to my debit card not working in Paraguay due to conflicting policies and the lack of pills to aid my dietary restriction of dairy within a country that uses dairy in almost every meal, I was going through it. In addition, I was in a Spanish speaking country where very few people spoke English aside from group-mates and two employees at the organization, [Paraguayan Social Enterprise], which we were working with. However, despite all of the obstacles, I had one of the best experiences of my life there and not so much from the project work or the impact we made on the company but for the personal experience I had.

For what Paraguay lacks in prestigious landscapes and tourism, it makes up for in hospitality and culture. For those seven weeks, I became Paraguayan, and that is something I loved the most. People would come up to me so excited and solely wanted to have conversations about where I'm from to American politics to discussing the history and culture of Paraguay. My Spanish rose from beginning level to intermediate within that short period of time by solely talking to the local people, engaging in conversations with the employee at the Laundromat each week, the employees at the supermarket, sharing the national dish, yerba maté, with a cab driver. After the first five weeks, I was so engrossed in the culture I was able to independently give my friend from Nigeria, who spoke zero Spanish, a trip to the Jesuit ruins of Paraguay in a far town away from our local home. There in Paraguay I tried food from Taiwan, Vietnam, Turkey, Brazil, and Germany, making friends with people from each place. In Paraguay, I was not American or Black or any other label/distinction. I was Lailah and I was family. The minute I stopped comparing Paraguay to America or reflecting on the bad luck I had encountered, I began to truly love and appreciate all that Paraguay had to offer. The trip confirmed the connection between my passion and career goals as well as illustrated my ability to adapt to change.

Brooklyn encrypted the love and appreciation of history, diversity, creativity, differences, and community in my soul since being a youth. Constantly being introduced to those of various backgrounds ranging in differences of socio-economic status, ethnicity, nationality, gender, sexual orientation, has led to my fascination with differences and understanding cultures outside of my own. Whether competitively swimming in a predominantly Polish neighborhood in Brooklyn where little emphasis is placed on my ethnicity or swimming varsity in college where a large emphasis is placed on one's differences, I've learned to value challenges and differences as opportunities for growth. Debates and discussions facilitate the exchange of ideas, thus providing opportunities to learn how and why others think a particular way. Adapting quickly to change, a previous weakness has turned into one of my biggest strengths. I enjoy working in a dynamic environment, engaging with people, and solving problems.

Fortunately, while working in the supply chain at [Snack Food Company], my passion and career intertwine. As an engineer, I love solving problems and making processes more efficient, but the most rewarding experience is building confidence and leadership in someone else. This aligns with my vision of becoming a leading executive of a multinational corporation, by way of supply chain and operations, to indirectly influence positive changes in developing countries and marginalized communities in the United States. I want to be a resource for others to use.

Aside from disadvantages due to historical events, a significant portion of the stagnant state of some developing countries is attributed to the lack of autonomy, collaboration, and consideration of cultural and environmental aspects within issues. For many international development projects, money is thrown to a problem, or a solution is given prior to full comprehension of the problem including consideration of multiple perspectives, especially cultural ones. This is one of the main factors why development projects fail. The people that tend to know the best solution to a problem are those of the community the problem impacts and require aid in the form of empowerment such as external consulting and resources so they can resolve their issues with a long-term sustainable solution.

My overall goal is to use my power and influence to facilitate projects and initiatives in developing countries that empower people to resolve the problems plaguing their community. Additionally, I aim to empower marginalized communities in the United States through increasing financial literacy, scholarship opportunities, facilitating the growth of small businesses and changes in policies. I want to give back to the neighborhood, Bedford-Stuyvesant in Brooklyn, NY, that has heavily invested much love, confidence, resources, and hope into me, by acquiring enough resources to buy back the area, which is currently undergoing rapid gentrification, and instead offer subsidized housing and property to low-income families and descendants of those who were forced out due to gentrification. I crave the ability to impact communities on a large scale and high level through policies, networking, and funding.

These goals are what brings me to Harvard. Everything I do is for all those looking up to me: my community relying on me and those communities seeking aid. I want to solve problems as an engineer, as a leader, and as a person. Harvard provides the challenge and environment most conducive to growth and preparation to accomplish these goals. So, who am I? My name is Lailah T. and I'm a young woman from Brooklyn, NY, trying to do my part in positively changing the world.

ANALYSIS

Lailah successfully conveys her love for her community and adaptability to change in her essay. In her introduction, Lailah opens with an engaging anecdote about a trip to Paraguay that, despite its initial challenges, served as a turning point during which she realized the link between her love for understanding cultures and her professional ambitions. Right from the start, Lailah makes use of an optimistic, engaging tone that effectively reflects the rest of her essay to admissions officers.

Lailah then explores these two points extensively within the body of the essay. Picking up the thread from her anecdote on Paraguay,

Lailah alludes to how her background in Brooklyn influenced some of her most defining strengths and characteristics as a person in business. Lailah then moves on to communicate how these characteristics align with her career history and aspirations for the future. Through her experience and knowledge of working with communities in need, Lailah showcases to admissions officers both positive determination and a pragmatic approach to her goals.

Lailah brings her essay to a close by summarizing how all these distinct elements have brought her to choose Harvard Business School. By citing the challenge and optimal environment for growth that Harvard could provide, Lailah brings to admissions officers her readiness for academic rigor and to her essay a compelling finish.

—Hiewon Ahn

CONCLUSION

As demonstrated throughout this book, the essay is one of the most crucial elements to your application, as one of few opportunities to show the admissions office who you are beyond the confines of your resume and test scores. While all fifty essays are written by individuals with entirely different experiences, each essay contains a compelling story about what has led them to apply to Harvard Business School. The admissions office wants to see who you are as a person, what values you stand for, and the dreams that you hope to someday achieve.

There is no cookie-cutter response for a successful HBS application essay. With that being said, here are five tips to help you craft your own successful HBS essay.

1. Bridge Your Nonbusiness-Related Identity to Your Business-Related Identity

While it may be difficult to think about what exactly sets you apart from other competitive applicants, it is important to remember that every facet of your identity is relevant to who you are and what you contribute to your communities. The Admissions Committee is interested in understanding who you are, and it is up to you to show how your experiences make you a great fit.

> No one has a perfect life story. Failures are normal and not every career move can be perfect; embrace this and show what you learnt each time things did not go your way. Learning is as important as achieving.
>
> —Siddharth J.

Do not feel pressure to hide your flaws or glamorize your life experiences. Instead, find a story that resonates with HBS vision and ideals.

No single application is perfect. Share your vulnerabilities openly and how the calluses of the past make you a whole person. Oftentimes, we obfuscate our flaws because we think that will make us a better candidate, but remember that everyone else is doing the same. Covering for fear of rejection only makes you another drop in the bucket. How you evolve and improve is a task that only you can show and tell and it is one of the only facets in your life that make you a different person.

—Leonardo L.

It is up to you to best show how your experiences have led you to become a great fit for Harvard Business School. Ask yourself how your experiences have shaped your core values and how you can craft a narrative around those stories. How do these values relate to who you would be in the HBS community, and later in the global community? Effectively bridging these aspects of your identity with Harvard Business School will enable you to clearly demonstrate the diversity of thought you are bringing to the table.

2. Call to HBS-Specific Opportunities

In such a competitive field with so many applicants and so few spots, it is incredibly important to be clear about why you want to attend business school and why you specifically want to attend Harvard Business School. Ultimately, the admissions process is about determining whether you are the right fit for the school. To demonstrate that fit, you must really understand what makes Harvard

Business School the MBA program that it is. This may take the form of discussing specific programs or professors that you are interested in, or mentioning other opportunities uniquely found at Harvard Business School. Your knowledge about the school may also be implicit and subtly demonstrated throughout your writing.

> Find out which business school is the best fit for you by doing tons of research and talking to as many people as possible. Then focus on reflecting upon your experiences in life and telling your own unique story. HBS's mission is to educate leaders who make a difference in the world. Leadership can be defined in many ways and reflect deeply upon what difference you want to make in the world!
> —Cecilia X.

Either way, it is extremely important to research precisely why you believe Harvard Business School is the right fit for you and what role your time at HBS will play in helping you achieve your broader goals in life and business.

3. Be Specific About Your Achievements

Harvard Business School values "habit of leadership," "analytical aptitude and appetite," and "engaged community citizenship." Although your resume lists your accomplishments, the Admissions Committee looks to your essay to construct a full picture of you as an applicant with these three qualities in mind. While writing your essay, strike the balance between presenting your accomplishments and humility.

Really look deeper at the MBA programs you are applying to. Go beyond the brand name, rankings, average starting salary, and alumni who have attended. Try to understand the culture of the institution and what classes, programs, and people fit into your MBA objectives. I found in-person visits really help here, but many schools have provided digital resources, including videos of classroom discussions and student programs, student and alumni stories, and speeches and panels from students and faculty on their websites. Really try to understand what motivates people to attend this specific institution, what the classroom dynamics are, how students and faculty interact to build consensus on ideas and learn frameworks.

—Sabrina F.

While sharing your experiences, introduce your core values and detail your impact concisely. Then, use your narrative to highlight what you wish to achieve through your experience at Harvard Business School.

4. Define Your Aspirations and Craft a Narrative That Explains Their Origins

Every applicant has an aspiration that they hope to realize through admission to Harvard Business School. Be sure to clearly define what makes your goals unique. Whether you dream of leading a start-up or joining an investment bank, think about how your aspirations connect to your core values.

The most important part of the essay is to think and reflect about what you want to do. I worked through several drafts of my essay over the course of ~2 months. I wrote and "finalized" a draft and ended up changing my whole essay last minute to reflect more of my voice and story. I was scared about showcasing my authentic self and voice, yet that is what I believe helped me stand out. I thought to myself, "If I could only tell HBS one thing, what would it be?" When I thought about this answer I realized my original essays were too formulaic; I needed to share the story of the people most important to me and weave that into how it's shaped my life. I'm very proud of my essay, but it took a long period of self-reflection to get it right.

—Adriana G.

Make sure to outline how Harvard Business School fits into this story. What do you hope to gain from your years at HBS? How will your leadership in the HBS community and the resources they have to offer fit into your plans for the future?

5. Ensure Your Voice Is Authentic and Direct

Beyond anything else, make sure that your admission essay is authentic. Do not try to be anyone you are not in your essay. While it may be tempting to overstate your accomplishments or to promise magnificent goals about the future, this is not what the HBS Admissions Committee is looking for.

Your personal statement is essentially a call to action. It is a statement designed to get an immediate response from the person reading it. In this context, it is a statement designed to get the admissions team to want to admit you. Your stats, your work experience, and other facets of your application may illustrate the strength of your candidacy, but it is the personal statement that will make the reader want to admit you. Give them the reason to do so. Provide them with the arguments so that they can go to their peers in the admissions team and advocate on your behalf.

But most importantly, don't tell them what you think they want to hear. Instead, be true to yourself and write what matters most to you.

—Kevin R.

Have confidence in yourself. Being honest with yourself as you write the essay makes you more interesting to the reader and helps them understand who you are beyond the statistics and resume. The question is open-ended for a reason: ultimately, they want to know what you would like them to know. Best of luck.

ABOUT *THE HARVARD CRIMSON*

The Harvard Crimson has been the daily newspaper of Harvard University since 1873. Published from Cambridge, Massachusetts, *The Crimson* is the nation's oldest continually operating daily college newspaper.